Mashangu's Reverie

Mashangu's Reverie
and other essays

N. Chabani Manganyi

RAVAN PRESS
Johannesburg

Published by Ravan Press, 60 Juta Street, Braamfontein, Johannesburg 2001

© Copyright N. Chabani Manganyi 1977

First impression November 1977

ISBN 0 86975 068 2 (hard cover)   0 86975 072 0 (soft cover)

Cover design: Selwyn Griffiths

All characters and incidents in the essay 'Mashangu's Reverie' are fictitious.

Printed by Zenith Printers (Pty) Ltd
60 Juta Street, Braamfontein, Johannesburg 2001

Contents

Preface

There was in the beginning of my encounter with America a gross kind of suffering which was gradually transformed into angry anguish. So overwhelming were the fantasies of revenge, so terrifying in their stark clarity, that it became important for me to arrive at some internal resolution of the diverse impulses which were constantly invading my consciousness. I started to write *Mashangu's Reverie,* which may be seen as a frivolous kind of 'self-analysis' and in this way started to rid myself of disturbing impulses. Writing about them transformed them from the realm of the personal to that of the universal.

Mashangu's Reverie was conceived and written during my stay at Yale University in New Haven, Connecticut. It was during those years that my unconscious as an inner and in a sense hidden self presented itself fully for the first time. Several reasons accounted for this achievement. One was the free and stimulating environment of the Yale academic community, the other the vicissitudes of living and being part of an intense psycho-therapeutic culture.

The first part of this collection of essays is a story of joy and sorrow. It represents for me a gut-level reaction to my experience as a black man in a social world created by white people primarily for their own ends. *Mashangu's Reverie* is to be viewed as a product of a psycho-analytically informed imagination grappling with *fragments of a stream of consciousness*. Fragments of this kind are useful to the extent that they mirror for us the kinds of existential dilemmas which confront members of subordinate groups. A study of the fragments as process, movement at various levels of consciousness, should not fail to isolate the struggles involved here. In extreme conditions of superordinacy and subordinacy, the *hero* in the latter case is the man or woman who thrives on the mask of sanity, whose individuality suffers from chronic internal divisions and whose existence is invaded by an experience of inauthenticity. There should be no doubt about the fact that the *double* who creates in the psyche of this hero the conditions essential for the flourishing of a false consciousness (inauthenticity) is an offshoot of violence to the self. This means that under conditions of subordinacy, the self that is projected in everyday life is false and unauthentic since it remains a mask protecting its double — an unnatural division which does violence to the integrity of the self.

Violence to the self is made lethal to one's individuality since it exists in equal proportion to the violence experienced as emanating from one's environment and in the ensuing cross-fire is turned into a consciousness of ambivalence. Ambivalence and its psychological, that is, behavioural, ramifications, in so far as these involve the resolution of the impulse to violence either against the self or others is the main theme of the essay: the *Violent Reverie*. The two *(The Violent Reverie* and *Mashangu's Reverie)* should be seen as separate though thematically related. The comments which follow are, therefore, relevant to both these essays.

It seems that violence as ideation, impulse or social act is difficult to fathom unless we widen the scope for the search of its sources, its ramifications and its resolution to include the unconscious (private subjective experience) which, in lay opinion at least, is equated with the realm of the irrational. I believe the unconscious and the primacy in human life of subjective experience are studied to the best advantage not only in dream life but also in literature and therapy in-depth (particularly through the psychoanalytic technique of free association).

The data for this study of the violent reverie and ambivalence arise from personal experience. There is a sense in which the fragments which formed themselves into the story in the first part of this book are autobiographical. Mind you, autobiographical not in the sense of factuality of events or situation but in the sense that the fragments are a free production of my consciousness including most that was unconscious but seeking recognition and expression. It may well be that some useful insight may be gained in respect of the subjective struggles around anger, resentment and violent impulses as well as the conditions essential for conflict resolution.

What started as a journey into my own subjective experience developed at a later stage into an intellectual curiosity about the origins of the impulse to violence either as fantasy or social act. It should become clear from a study of the two separate but related essays that one of the most excruciating dilemmas facing subordinates is the need at one time or another to come to terms with the violent reverie in its many unconscious disguises — the fantasy about killing and being killed.

Differences in theme between the essays that deal directly with the many faces of violence and the other essays in this collection are more apparent than real. This is so since we are to see later that violence is not to be understood only as social act but also as fantasy as well as the various forms of insult to the dignity of man. The final judgement, of course, remains the reader's. I need only add without too full an anticipation of what is to follow that the problem of violence in most societies today is an important one. Like all important human challenges, it occupies both national and international spheres of concern. To read Koestler's *Darkness at Noon* and Maurice Merleau-Ponty's somewhat unsympathetic critique of what he (Merleau-Ponty) so teasingly describes as 'Koestler's dilemmas' is to come face to face with the challenge of violence as human reality. It must be remembered that although both authors concern themselves mainly with a searching examination of violence within the overall promise of communism, they tell us a great deal about violence in the ordering of human societies. This important insight of Merleau-Ponty's in his *Humanism and Terror* needs to be established once and for all and here we need to go to the source to be reminded and perhaps guided:

When one is living in what Peguy called an historical *period,* in which political man is content to administer a regime or an established law, one can hope for a history without violence. When one has the misfortune or the luck to live in an *epoch,* or one of those moments where the traditional ground of a nation or society crumbles and where, for better or for worse, man himself must reconstruct human relations, then the liberty of each man is a mortal threat to the others and violence reappears.

(And a little later)

We must remember that liberty becomes a false ensign — a 'solemn complement' of violence — as soon as it becomes only an ideal and we begin to defend liberty instead of free men. It is then claimed that humanity is being preserved despite the miseries of politics; in reality, and at this very moment, one is endorsing a limited politics. It is the essence of liberty to exist only in the practice of liberty, in the inevitably imperfect movement which joins us to others, to the things of the world, to our jobs, mixed with the hazards of our situation. In isolation, or understood as a principle of discrimination, like the law according to St. Paul, liberty is nothing more than a cruel god demanding his hecatombs. An aggressive liberalism exists which is a dogma and already an ideology of war. It can be recognised by its love of the empyrean principles, its failure ever to mention the geographical and historical circumstances to which it owes its birth, and its abstract judgements of political systems without regard for the specific conditions under which they develop. Its nature is violent, nor does it hesitate to impose itself through violence in accordance with the old theory of the secular arm.

Following Peguy's distinction then we might say that many societies today are living through historical epochs in that in many of them 'man himself must reconstruct human relations.' Southern Africa is no exception in this respect since it is in this part of the world that the reconstruction of race relations must occur.

One need not define violence so broadly that the definition becomes meaningless. But on the other hand, the phenomenon we are now considering appears in so many forms in different historical and social contexts that this generality of the phenomenon in human relations must always be captured irrespective of the narrowness or comprehensiveness of one's conception of violence. Amin's Uganda has been singled out recently as being one of the most violent societies in the world today. According to one view of violence (a view limited to a corpse count) Amin's Uganda may well be the most violent of societies today. If this view of violence were the only one which needed consideration other manifestations of violence would certainly be ignored. To be violent, a society need not have several thousand corpses to its national credit. Indeed, societies do become violent and have become violent in the past in pursuit of a 'non-violent' way of life. This historical paradox arises the moment the fear of potential violence becomes so strong that it creates violence, believing it to be necessary to prevent potential violence from being made manifest in the society. This paradox, it should be added, is the central dilemma of the dictator and his regime.

In addition to the study of violence on the level of 'publics' we need an appreciation of how individuals in the privacy of their lives experience violence as a human reality. Some of the essays which follow are written from the perspective of the individual and his vicissitudes in the face of experienced violence. Indeed, where liberty becomes an abstract principle and not a basis for the experience and ordering of freedom the individual comes face to face with violence.

NOEL CHABANI MANGANYI
University of Transkei
November 1977.

PART I

Mashangu's Reverie

Mashangu's Reverie

'Well, Dr Mashangu, we have fifty minutes on our side. Please tell me how I can help you.' A moment of silence followed. Mashangu, clearing his voice and shifting in his chair, broke the silence and said in a low monotone: 'I would ... really be hard put if I were to tell you in a few words. Each time I think about it, my problems seem to be so different each time. Let's say I am unhappy. I don't know ... I do know, however, I've been unhappy on and off — in the dumps as they say.' Mashangu pronounced his words as if he was feeling his way. He lapsed into an introspective silence.

Dr Davies, the therapist, regarded him with an air of benevolence. He spoke with such composure that each word and phrase felt like a startling intrusion into Mashangu's private world. Mashangu pulled himself together to hear Dr Davies' voice come out clearly yet gently: 'Could you tell me when it was that you first recognised this unhappiness as something for which you required professional help?'

'How I wish I could tell,' replied Mashangu with notable hesitation. For a moment he felt confused by what he sensed as an invitation to be drawn out into the open arena.

'I knew the moment I walked in here ... the moment I could find a chair, that the big Shrink's past-time would become an issue ... my past. What about it?' he finished with a touch of irritation. His voice was rising to a tremor muffled by the swift shifts in his feelings in the consulting office. Dr Davies would not be drawn out.

'Well, where does one begin?' inquired Mashangu.

'As you please,' responded Davies with unnerving confidence. He continued: 'We must appreciate that it is important for me to know as much as you can tell before I can know in what ways I may be helpful.'

'I'll tell you everything. Everything.'

No sooner had Mashangu said 'everything' than he felt a need to qualify the statement, regaining some composure as he did.

'I was born in South Africa during the last world war. Coming to think about it, that is how I picked up the names George and Churchill which I dropped as soon as I knew how. By the way, do I have to present this in chronological order?'

'As you wish,' said Davies almost instinctively.

'Ah, I promised to tell everything, didn't I?'

Mashangu waited expectantly for Davies to say something. Davies continued to mouth his pipe as though there was nothing the matter.

'I was born in South Africa. It is important to repeat this. I was born in rural South Africa . . . I mean rural. You are not likely to understand.'

'Proceed all the same,' said Davies encouragingly.

'I was born in a country village — a chief's kraal — royal blood. My father declined chieftainship several times. The reasons have always been obscure but I think he treasured his life. I was the only child of my father's first marriage. My father married a second wife when I was about eight. He got married to a niece of my mother's. I remember that the marriage negotiations took a long time. Retrospectively, I must have rejoiced at the prospect of company — brothers and sisters, perhaps. It may sound strange to you. The first six years of my life I spent with mother, father only coming home during Christmas. He worked in Johannesburg, I was told. Apart from the local trading store, there was a one-classroom school in our village. I attended that school for one year. I remember the morning fights we used to have with mother when I did not feel like going to school. Sometimes she would raise hell and spank me . . . kind of gracefully. That was her manner.'

He stopped suddenly and looked thoughtful as he searched his pockets for cigarettes. He lit one and puffed away nervously. Dr Davies looked at his watch as Mashangu started to smoke silently. He put his pipe into a huge ashtray on the low table with the appearance of wanting to emerge fully from his corner.

'I notice that we have a few minutes before the end of our hour. I do want to say that we have an unusual situation here. It is bound to affect the ways in which I may be helpful or not. Eeh, we're likely to need more time than usual talking things over in a preliminary way. Our backgrounds are different, you see. You grew up in a culture completely foreign to me. But, and here lies the important issue, we may turn a stumbling block into an opportunity and a challenge. If it's okay by you I suggest we meet a few more times before deciding on a definite course of action. That should give us a chance to assess the helpful potential of the situation. In this way we leave open the question whether we wish to work together. That should give me a chance to decide whether your difficulties are of such a nature as to be resolved through psychotherapy. How do you feel about what I've suggested thus far, eh?'

Mashangu had been attentive all the while. Yet he was conscious of having scrutinised Davies' every movement, gesture, change in facial expression as well as the inflections of his voice. Once Mashangu had indicated consent, Davies continued:

'Let's see,' he said thumbing through his schedule. 'How about meeting twice a week? We'll shift the time around to suit us both, okay?'

Once the times had been settled Davies said:

'We'll meet at the appointed times for exactly fifty minutes each time. I recommend that appointments be kept as far as is humanly possible. If for any reason you are unable to come, please call me in good time. I'll do likewise. It is also a necessary condition for the work to progress to limit our working time to this office and the times scheduled for our sessions. These are my expectations. One last thing before we finish off. All that I will expect of you on coming to therapy sessions is that you talk about what is uppermost in your mind . . . what occurs to you at the time without any regard to its appropriateness. What you say or do not say, as it were, will be the material on which to

3

work. As you can imagine, you'll do most of the talking. I'll listen, talk a little sometime, ask a question here and there. Don't be surprised if I should not feel inclined to reply to some questions you might ask. It will depend upon the situation — whether I think replying will further our work or not. That is a mouthful for today, isn't it? I'm afraid our time is up now,' Davies said as he uncrossed his legs to stand up.

'Goodbye, Dr Mashangu,' Davies said as he opened the door for Mashangu who responded: 'Goodbye, Doctor.'

Mashangu walked out of the offices of the Mental Health Centre at five o'clock in the afternoon. A few paces along the silent corridor leading to the elevators and away from the common reception area, he thought about his experience that afternoon. All along the corridor were closed doors on each side with 'do not disturb' signs on them which helped transform the prison-like atmosphere into a sanitised professional one. Mashangu saw his surroundings clearly for the first time after his consultation with Dr Davies. Rather than indulge his fancy about the paintings hanging along the walls, he moved even faster towards the elevators. He had decided to drive to a favourite coffee house in College Street.

The drive was a short one. Once at the coffee house, Mashangu selected a secluded spot at the rear of the eating area. He had eaten here so often that once the waitress had seen him she indulged herself only to the extent of asking him whether he wanted 'the usual.' He nodded agreement as he made himself restful. Service was slow at that time but once the food had been brought, Mashangu could not enjoy it. He liked the coffee though and he sipped it thoughtfully. He sipped so slowly that it was as if each sip was intended to correspond to one idea at a time.

Most prominent were recollections of his experiences at the Mental Health Centre. He remembered feeling confused — not knowing which chair to sit on. There had been a couch too along the wall. Everything else seemed blurred except for the figure of Dr Davies himself. Mashangu held himself in check vowing silently that he would not spend another second on that experience until his next appointment. That decision only served to bring him closer to his own little internal world.

It was a timeless world of heroes and heroines with a life of their own demanding to be heard and gain immortality in their own right. 'Loneliness is so idiomatic,' he repeated to himself in a soft whisper. As he prepared to leave the coffee house, he wished he were already in his apartment. The image of a foetus at full term ready to be evacuated into the world flashed through his mind as he paid his bill in readiness to drive to his apartment.

His desk at No. 650 College Street was awaiting him with the evidence of previous labours. On entering his room, a kind of studio apartment with bathroom, kitchenette, combined living and sleeping area, he went straight to his desk without taking off his winter coat. It was cluttered with books, papers and a pipe stand at one end with several pipes dangling from it. Mashangu scrounged around for his journal in readiness to make an entry for the day. That evening he made one of the longest entries, writing slowly at first:

NOVEMBER 9, 1974

'I, M. Mashangu, consulted a shrink for the first time, thousands of miles away from my native land — confusing. It is winter. Through this window, I can see the last remains of last week's snow-storm. The moods, sounds and smells of winter remind me of home-in-exile . . .

The Sun

prostituting its rays
seductively through a veil
in December
captures the South of Africa
in a surreptitious embrace
under a scowling sky.
Hopes of yesteryear
in the South in December
floated stealthily in rays of splendour yesterday.
Lo!
the North in December
floating scraggy leaves of snow
whirl and twirl and sting
to freeze the flicker

5

it will . . .
will not return to us in our prime.

'They say I am a thorn in the flesh — *swart gevaar*! They say I have a low I.Q. pseudospeciation! When I came to, when I came round to being myself, I was a gift to the universe . . . like you. I started on a pilgrimage of devotion. A devotion to salvage something from the debris . . . "we are in rat's alley" . . . a devotion to give the world something. I was a spirit-flesh soiling diapers in the fullness of spring. The sun dragged its feet going, I knew not where, while the moon clung tenaciously to a nightly kingdom star-speckled and sombre. When birds had followed the sun, I and the gentle ones; Mother's arms and a star-studded moon clung to a nightly kingdom in the promise of Spring. South Africa, my castle, is called a republic and was once a union. I, a pilgrim turned refugee in search of a gaping grave singing . . .

> the only thing you have ever owned
>> will ever own
> outside this consciousness that says
>> I — ME
> through a *tour de force* can say
>> you and them and it
> is a piece of land six feet deep
> I can't tell you where it's going to be
>> when it's going to be
> all I know is
> it's gotta be some place.

'A pilgrim turned refugee is exiled from history and participation — an apology. What remained of the pilgrim embraced a double-edged dagger and . . .

> in some instances
> little details make the day
> an important difference in the case of murder
> that was it . . . a murder
> the victim not a nondescrip
> a man in his prime
> at the prime of a civilisation
> Once the deed was done

Mother appeared unannounced
wielding a gentle reminder:
"My son
you were born at dawn one morning
snuff, jokes, three old ladies and anxious moments
whispers, my son
something to the effect that feet first an ominous sign
my son
you did better than Machaba
toddled with kittens and chicks
a delightful landmark in the homestead
you joined your peers herding cattle
ploughing the fields with your elders
it was not long
not long before you knew something about wild berries,
    snakes and birds
about questions of seniority
I Mwamkhaxani
Obeyed your father's instruction
to send you to a Mission School
it was there so you did tell me
where you learnt the alphabet under a sprouting fig tree
there
where there was something the teacher called being on
    time
somebody *Mfundisi* called Miss-something-or-other
Miss-something-or-other
God in person
carried a torch at all times
embering in the village 'darkness'
she and her kind told you about a God without siblings
about purity-white-virtue = God
an approach to grace
about scum-darkness — shame = Satan
a retreat from salvation
there
where they put one word into the bargain
one word —
the day you learnt to say yes . . . yes

7

it was the bold stroke
my son
I could tell more but wait!
a blood-stained dagger?
tell me . . . will you?"
I did
nothing certain
they tell me . . .
I believe it is
a murder . . . something radical
tore those robes to shreds
murder
a final no . . . no indeed
there, in his bath tub
I saw his cheeks heave
crying for mercy
killed a prime master
not a nondescript
said no on the sharp edge of a dagger
no, indeed . . .

'Today I say yes and no being ablaze with affirmation.'

Once Mashangu had written the last word, he thumped his
fist on the desk as a kind of signature to it all. Perhaps this
action on his part was metaphoric — a symbol of a successful
delivery. As he moved over to the kitchen to make himself some
coffee, he mused with a contented smile over the thought that
he had acted like a mid-wife after a successful delivery. He was
not feeling exhausted though he had been at it for some time.
What he felt was an invigorating mix of relief and alertness
such as to make him wonder whether sleep would come easily.
After coffee he undressed and jumped into bed without
pyjamas as was his habit.

It was important for him to fall asleep as fast as he could.
There were no classes to teach in the morning since there was to
be a faculty meeting at nine. Mashangu tried to make himself
comfortable by lying on his back while struggling to keep his
eyes closed. His determination to disregard the events of the
day was not immediately successful. A number of disconnected

thought-images kept creeping past his diminishing attention: Apartment 9C Victoria Towers ... New York Street ... perhaps Johannesburg ... black faces, hundreds of them ... police officers ... identity papers — 'dom pass' ... Oh my God! ... who was that black woman leading a child across the Street? ... Where-here-there-now? Yes ... space ... what does that mean, here now? here New York, yesterday, there Johannesburg ... here now 1974 ... Johannesburg, 1938 ... a little black boy herding cattle at Tshakhuma ... cattle and school and initiation and a white missionary ... a veritable pot pourri in this bed ... here and there and what of now? Now is quicksand ... unstable like that dream I had yesterday.

Mashangu's appetite for sleep was rewarded but not without experience having taken its toll.

The day following Mashangu's visit to the Mental Health Centre was sunny and windy. Walking through the paths and streets criss-crossing the old campus with its brooding ivy-covered structures, he waved to one student across the street and went his way. At that time of day, students and lecturers mingled in the doorways and streets leading from the university to the downtown area. Mashangu was in no mood to be jovial after a frustrating faculty meeting that morning. His walk became brisk as he approached a block of apartment dwellings on Crown Street in the downtown area. A friend had called to ask Mashangu for drinks before dinner and he had accepted promptly to satisfy a need for conversation with someone other than Dr Davies. Davies could wait until the following day. At University Towers, Mashangu pressed the bell knob for Chivuso's apartment. The main door to the hall-way opened instantly.

Chivuso lived on the seventh floor in elegant style. His apartment was spacious and lavishly furnished, so much so that his friends, Mashangu included, often accused him of decadence. Chivuso always took kindly to such jibes, often disarming his accusers with a peal of genial laughter. When Mashangu walked out of the elevator, he felt his mood lifting in spite of the familiar smells of communal living. He had not been to Chivuso's rooms, as they were called, for a while and it was with a sense of joyous anticipation that Mashangu knocked at 7B. Chivuso's beaming smile appeared in the doorway. A firm squeeze around the shoulders ushered the two friends into the living area. There was a lot of room between the leather chairs, cushions, stereo systems, books and paintings on the walls.

'Well, brother, what will it be this time? It's a long time since we had a drink together,' said Chivuso as he walked towards a cocktail cabinet sitting snugly in one corner.

'One never knows with you. Sometimes it's beer and you swear you can outdrink a Londoner on a hot summer's day. Is it one of those other days when you have more delicate tastes? . . . scotch on the rocks, eh?'

Mashangu regarded Chivuso carefully. He did not feel like drinking much that evening.

'It will be malt this time,' said Mashangu nonchalantly.

'Very well then, here we go,' retorted Chivuso, bringing a cold bottle of Heineken from the refrigerator. Putting the bottle and beer mug on a coffee table beside him, Mashangu lit a fresh cigarette.

Mashangu felt relaxed and warm. Yet he could not get himself to match Chivuso's high spirits. Chivuso, seeming to sense that something was amiss, began to inquire whether there was anything the matter.

'Nothing in particular,' replied Mashangu with assumed indifference.

'What is new on the home-front?' inquired Chivuso with a little more persistence in his voice.

'Nothing which you've not heard about on TV or read in the *Times*'. There was a brief silence before Mashangu started to talk again.

'I've not heard from home in a while. People there must survive as best they can. Letter-writing is a luxury, see?'

Chivuso prepared himself for a few more cynical remarks sipping his Cognac delicately from a big brandy-sniffer. He had got his friend started and was content merely to add that Nigerians in Lagos were in no way different.

'You know Chivuso, while you were going through the motions of asking me what I'd drink, I was thinking about the past. Let's say three or four years ago back home. Maybe, even a little earlier than that. We used to drink so much whisky you'd have thought we could all afford it. Psychologically, yes ... we deserved the scotch but certainly not financially. Women, lots of them were always in the picture too. They too were a psychological necessity. I remember Moshe used to say: "Brother, if morals don't serve me I throw them overboard." What do you know about life in Lagos today having lived abroad for such a long time? Apart from what you pick up in the Nigerian novel today you know very little about life in post-independence Nigeria.'

'Don't be so sure, I take a peep out there now and again,' protested Chivuso.

'Okay, ... but you have no idea what life is like in Soweto ... a black ghetto, something close to Harlem in Manhattan. Imagine for one moment about a million black people of all ages. Black souls, my dear fellow, with literally nothing to do between five in the afternoon when they leave white Johannesburg until some return as early as four in the morning. Gospel truth, I tell you. Thousands of men and women evacuated each day from the city to face the ugly darkness of life in the location. Of course ... little loves here and there, festering bitterness all round. Look Chivuso, I didn't pay you a visit just to gossip about South Africa.'

'You may not feel like talking about your country. Your reticence is fully appreciated. Yet I believe there are many people who would scoff at what you've just said. They would say: he's a militant so-and-so suffering from an inflamed imagination.'

'That's hog-wash Chivuso. You've heard it all before ... the stuff about counter-racism, radicals, anarchists and communists, haven't you?'

Chivuso stood up to refill his glass and bring Mashangu a fresh bottle of beer. Mashangu topped his beer mug and waited. His mind was poignantly active. Unleashed at that time were memories, feelings and ideas which he condensed into images. When he started to talk, Chivuso recognised that passion in Mashangu's voice and eyes which he admired so much.

'Munghana wami,' Mashangu started with deliberate ease,

11

'there is no place for truth anymore. There was a time when there was something you could call public truth, public morality, collective ideals. Faith, yes . . . it also was once a public commodity. What you and I have to-day is subjective, personal, idiomatic — something which at best is self-sustaining inside. Something is true only to the extent that it is self-sufficient, needing nothing external to it. Once it becomes public . . . it becomes formless and false because public vulgarity forms around it.' Mashangu stopped suddenly to find himself a cigarette. He flipped one out and lit it, drawing heavy puffs which formed thick clouds of smoke around his face.

Chivuso said in his usual jovial manner: 'There are many issues about which we are at odds. You'll say it's frivolous but I'll give it all the same. Take my lack of ambivalence about white broads. Maybe I am ambivalent, but I've never taken the time to think about it. You see, I follow a simple impulse . . . see it to the very end. Simple isn't it? I think it is simple until one adopts the attitude of those who feel blacks should account for every choice they make. The scrutiny comes from all directions.'

'How about blaming the victim? . . . it's our fault,' insisted Mashangu. The statement felt emphatic and Mashangu admired this sense of conviction in himself. He continued:

'You may not agree but I think we are responsible for our feeling of perpetual victimisation. We've missed many historical opportunities and are still paying for those gross errors of judgment. Now there are other opportunities — a chance for black people to project new visions. Whether we like it or not, mankind is clutching at sterile straws; trying to build a civilisation out of garbage spewed during the past three centuries or so. I think it was T. S. Eliot who wrote something like: the world revolves like ancient women gathering fuel in vacant lots. The futility of it all . . . Can you see Africa making a contribution in the urgent rescue work? The black man must stop feeling victimised. He must stand out straight, tall and clearly.'

The phone started to ring. Chivuso went to answer it. 'Chivuso' his voice boomed out, suggesting mild irritation. 'Yes, hi!' he responded. 'Nothing in particular. Just having a drink before dinner with a friend . . . Who? . . . Mashangu. He's been here for a while . . . from Johannesburg, South Africa . . . yeah . . . We plan to go to the Old for dinner. Well, do hop along. He won't mind . . . He may even like you . . . Okay, till then.' He hung up.

'That was Okike. I don't think you've met Okike. Quite a chick! . . . Women are not your bag . . . are they? I thought you'd show some curiosity — some interest. The artist, of course . . .'

'I've not published anything yet. Nothing substantive. You know I keep a journal but it may all come to nothing in the end. Isn't that a familiar story? The journal is mine you see . . . mine . . . It is not a public document. It is not yet vulgar. I keep control over it, I nourish it daily and my personal truth sheds light through its pages.'

Mashangu finished his last helping of beer much faster than Chivuso had expected. They started on their way to the Old. It was early evening and the sky was overcast. The streets were humming with traffic in all directions. They shared jokes as they walked along interrupted by Chivuso who would land his eyes on some of the passing women.

It was about seven when they reached their destination. Chivuso, efficient in such matters, immediately requested a table for three as they were being ushered into the main dining area. Members of the academic community dined and drank at the Old each day. The dining area was separated from a bar by a small waiting area with seats on both sides of the connecting corridor. Beyond the waiting area, the dining area had an air of contrived intimacy about it. People who had escaped the confines of their own houses and apartments could be seen hanging winter coats and gathering unwieldy long evening dresses in preparation for dinner. Away from the darker recesses with tables for couples were tables for groups larger than three. The myriad of secrets, disappointments, fulfilled and suffocating passions which must have floated through that area are matters for one's imagination. The Old, as the name suggests, was one of the oldest restaurants in town. Successive owners had retained the ancient atmosphere of the place not merely for aesthetic reasons but also to recover the shrinking buying power of the dollar. Along its walls were exotic paintings and pictures. An old accumulation of dust on these and other ornaments had become less obtrusive with time.

Chivuso and Mashangu were offered a table away from the nests reserved for couples. From where they sat, they could see people coming in and leaving.

'This is sure a good vantage point to see Okike waltz in,' said Chivuso as he took a chair.

'My lady when she walks treads on the ground,' interposed Mashangu facetiously.

He continued: 'You seem to be as fastidious about females as you are about those collector's pieces which adorn your rooms. I must say, what intrigues me is not your enthusiasm for women but the ability to sustain it . . . stick it out to the end. I mean: the end is always some kind of bathos, a let down. I've known you to go beyond that with your 'cuties' as you often so lustfully describe them . . . to limbo. Sometimes, mark you . . . I've envied you.'

So interested were they in this conversation that they had failed to notice the waitress who had come to take their orders. She had waited for them to notice her, to feel her feminine presence. When they failed her, she announced herself unmistakably: 'May I take your orders please? . . . Any cocktails?'

Chivuso and Mashangu looked up instantly.

'Well, well,' started Chivuso, 'actually it will be another fifteen minutes before we eat. We're waiting for a young lady to join us. Cocktails would suit us fine for the moment. Mashangu, what will you have? I'll have a dry sherry.'

'A bloody-mary please . . .'

The waitress left for a brief moment and returned with their drinks. As she placed their drinks on the table an attractive African woman walked into view. It was Okike.

She was not exactly what the commercial world would call a bomb-shell or sex symbol. In her dress, manner and body configuration she appeared to defy description and explode beyond stereotypes. There was something about her, a quality; a feeling tone which spelt freshness each time one looked at her. She wore these graces with the utmost indifference, enveloping

14

herself with an ease of manner and childlike spontaneity. One had to get closer to her to feel the full magnitude of her beauty.

Okike spotted Chivuso quickly and hurried to their table. As she approached the table, both Mashangu and Chivuso stood up. Mashangu and Okike were introduced to each other and the party settled down to dine. They got to know a little more about each other, where they had come from and what they were each doing at the university. Mashangu could not pay much attention to the chit-chat about Watergate, the Middle East and the local theatre season. He was uncomfortable and selfconscious about it. For long stretches at a time, his eyes would settle on Okike. She, for her part, was paying attention to him, engaging him in the chit-chat and regarding him warmly and affectionately. He was engrossed with her gestures and utterances.

Soon after dinner Mashangu excused himself by saying that he had some work to do that night. They moved out of the restaurant together to take Okike to her car. She bade them farewell, expressing a wish to meet them again soon. The two men walked together part of the way.

When Mashangu walked into his apartment it was eleven o'clock. He looked around the desolate room as though he expected to find someone awaiting him. For the first time since he had lived there he wished there was someone to talk to. He moved aimlessly around the narrow confines of his apartment thinking about that African woman from West Africa. He must be infatuated he thought to himself as he took several steps towards the phone. 'Sleep over it . . . sleep over it,' he heard himself murmuring to the cold emptiness of his room. The thought of coffee and an entry in his journal revived him as though there was some magic about his journal. He made himself a mug-full of black coffee and positioned himself at his desk with a pipe full of tobacco to make an entry in his journal:

NOVEMBER 10, 1974

'Went to a faculty meeting — insipid. Led a seminar on Camus — exciting. Had dinner with my Nigerian friend Chivuso and lo! I made a new acquaintance with a charming lady — the object of my passion — lust? The Myth of Sisyphus for me is the beginning of an important question.

'Sisyphus is the absurd hero. Pushing the rock uphill is the price I pay . . . for what? I am not Camus, nor am I the West. I the black Sisyphus am social — not metaphysical. It is the social which constitutes the horizon of my futile labour. Going downhill I come face to face with the social — my tormentors. I make the only logical jump I know, ie ignoring suicide in favour of something so painfully pragmatic — murder. As I take my breath, it is not so much the rock but my social tormentors who are at the helm of my consciousness. Suicide is no longer an option.

'I did . . . did not participate in the rebellion of the West. Yet I carry the burden of the questions they raised. As I and you emerge into the universe, it is no longer silent. I and you are forced to confront the ugly question of murder. Is it still possible to begin with innocence? Damn William Blake!'

Mashangu remained seated at his desk, smoking. When he stood up with an audible yawn the image of Okike reappeared with a new intensity. He was going to indulge himself. He would do something irregular. After all, he thought, he was seeing a shrink. He decided to give her a call even though it was late at night. Flipping over the pages of the Book of Names, he found her name and number and phoned her.

Mashangu took his life seriously. All of it: its ugliness included. He felt so close to life as to survive the most extreme of situations. It had not been the events in their circumscribed specificity that enthralled him. Rather it was his decision to use experience, to integrate it into his being. Ugliness had showed its face. He internalised it together with the illusions of his youth. Seeing a therapist and keeping a journal had a desperate quality about them. Mashangu was involved in a fervent attempt at recovering his past as the royal road to the future. His past was buried beneath his footsteps and appeared even more precious for that reason. The artisitic impulse in him was an act of retrieval and self-creation.

Anybody who knew him could hardly fail to sense that there was some quality which cut him out for a man apart. It seemed always to be a quality which found expression in his eyes, an impression of depth and a lingering profundity of penetration.

Women, choosing pragmatism over metaphysics, always described this quality as a phallic gaze. He was handsome without the fine line of feature and proportion characteristic of some effeminate homosexuals.

It was the day following his frantic call to Okike. He had managed after initial hesitation on her part to convince her to accept an invitation for dinner.

The day felt somewhat unusual for him. Mashangu experienced a fresh sense of vitality anchored in wild and random erotic fantasies. This was all in anticipation of his dinner engagement with Okike on Sunday. His self-indulgence was rudely curtailed when he realised that he had only forty minutes left before his appointment with Dr Davies. He looked around his office for reading material for the night and left to keep his appointment with Davies.

Dr Davies saw his private patients at the Mental Health Centre. Apart from his clinical responsibilities, he supervised therapists in training and was dedicated to serious intellectual pursuits. He was engaging his mind with certain substantive questions. If pressured, he would grudgingly say that he practised psychoanalytic psychotherapy. In practice, however, he was guided by the unique situation between himself and his patient. His views on the contribution of culture to neurotic and other psychological malformations were well known. It was with these beliefs as a baseline that he would sit in therapy and relate to his patients, aware of the contributions of biography and collective history. In discussions with students and colleagues, Davies could be heard proclaiming that behind every disorder which emerges during the course of a life and in therapy can be found a related public issue. His friends, more often than not, accused him of sitting on the fence between matters individual and those which were purely social.

Although he viewed Mashangu's treatment as a challenge to be met, it was also true that he felt some uneasiness because he had no experience with black patients, least of all an African. In the five minute interval between his last client and Mashangu, Davies sat in his office trying to refresh his memory about South Africa. This dull reverie was intercepted by the muffled ring of his phone. It was the secretary announcing

Mashangu's arrival. Davies stood up and buttoned his jacket to meet Mashangu at the reception area.

When they arrived in the office, Mashangu re-experienced the confusing feeling of his first visit. Once he had sat down, he wondered why he had chosen the same chair that he had used during his first visit. Davies looked at him expectantly. Mashangu crossed one leg over the other but felt uncomfortable immediately.

'Well, well, where do we go from here?' asked Mashangu rhetorically.

'I was just reminiscing over our last session here.'

He stopped suddenly as if to assess the impact of what he had just said. It had always seemed to him that he could never lose his self-possession nor his dedication to clear statement. Mashangu tried to find his way through the anger and surprise which were beclouding his judgement and said:

'I . . . I was trying to recollect the point at which I left off. My memory is good, on the average, that is. Yet for a moment, it seemed all blank. I remember what happened after our consultation more vividly.'

Fingering a cigarette and tapping it on the edge of the ashtray, playing at removing ash which had not yet started to form, Mashangu went silent for a moment. Then he broke the silence to say:

'The evening after the first appointment, I made some entries in my journal. I do that every day as a matter of course. It was a remarkable entry.'

Davies said in a soft, almost cultivated tone:

'Please tell me about that remarkable entry.'

'As I see it now, it's really of no consequence. It seemed important when I wrote it. If you were of an artistic bent you'd understand. An artistic creation . . . say a poem, takes on a life of its own the moment it's brought into being. No matter how much the artist tries, he is unable to recapture the creative impulse and experience which brought the product into being. It's more like giving away parts of oneself during the peak of orgasm . . . something one is unable to sustain for a long time. The whole entry had a nostalgic flavour to it . . . Oh yes, there was some political stuff . . . a kind of dream or fantasy about a political assassination of an important political figure. I told you something about my youth, right? Early experiences and later ones ... the sheer impossibility of innocence in adulthood. Does that make sense? You know, I was sent to a Mission School about eighty miles away from home. I must have been about seven and it was the year of the great drought, 1947 to be exact. I stayed with a maternal uncle; father to my second mother. He had two wives, three sons and two daughters.

'He died ... poor fellow, after a short illness. I remember the ominous cloud of silence that descended on his household following his death. I recall that distinctly. People, relatives and neighbours, came and went silently communing only with the wisdom of darkness and death. After his death ... oh! rivalries and accusations in the air. My uncle's wives were at each other's throats. I went to the mission school and herded cattle, goats and sheep across the Letaba river in the afternoons.

'What a fiasco! ... I almost drowned in that dreadful river one afternoon. Imagine ... A young man, a boy trying to learn something from the shepherd culture the same time that he was learning about the alphabet and Joseph the Dreamer.'

Suddenly Mashangu seemed to lose interest in his recollections. Here he was telling the story of his life to an American. 'Why' he asked himself silently.

The silence brought something in its wake — memories and experiences which had seemed irretrievably lost appeared in dazzling vividness in Mashangu's mind. All the sounds of distant insects, birds and the smells of country grass and cowdung glutted his consciousness. The school house of his youth reappeared to him in faint whitewash behind the Mission House where a stocky white chaplain used to live. She had lived there, so it had seemed, coming from some distant land to that remote village to superintend the souls of the local 'primitives.' Mashangu glanced at one of his finger nails. It still bore the marks of an accident involving the school bell that used to hang ponderously from the branch of a fig tree in the school-yard.

Dr Davies left Mashangu to his silence. He watched Mashangu's postural changes; the distracted expression on his face that changed without warning to one of intense concentration. Davies had listened attentively and had allowed part of his attention to stay close to Mashangu's experience of his recollections. Since it appeared to Davies that Mashangu could benefit from encouragement, he started to talk in a supportive tone. That surprised Mashangu and made him feel nervous.

'You've been silent for a while now. Please tell me what's been going through your mind.'

Mashangu, disappointed because Davies had not said much more, looked at the time.

'Many things occurred to me,' replied Mashangu in a hostile tone.

'Indeed!'

Mashangu discovered that he was paying less attention to what he was saying as his voice rose to an awkward tremor in pitch.

'How should I expect you to understand?

'I . . . I was thinking of repudiation. You know what I mean? Repudiation. I was looking at my life since the days at the Mission School. It has been one big battle repudiating, negating something or other — myself, my culture even my people. You see, we're forced to speak only English on certain days at school. Mind you, not only to enable us to read Milton or Shakespeare at a later stage but to prepare us . . . to create in us a readiness to repudiate everything which was native to us. Can you visualise that . . . each one of us carries a double . . . a kind of replica of self that is always in conflict with the mask that faces the world. To protect this mask from its double, one cherished an illusion and nourished it — the illusion that the future and prosperity of the mask depends upon a negation of the past both individual and collective . . .'

When Mashangu stopped talking, time was almost up. They both seemed to sense this for they continued in silence for a little while Davies felt that he was surviving the initial thrusts of hostility from his patient. There were other feelings which Davies experienced as still unformed. After Mashangu had left, Dr Davies stuffed his pipe with deliberate ease as he thought about their encounter. Working through his feelings in that hour, it occurred to him that what he had experienced was a vague sense of being provoked. He had felt as if Mashangu was calling him out, setting him up to shoulder the burden of a white South African. It had also felt like an accusation but he would not let Mashangu suck him in.

Africans living in the United States may be found scattered in small pockets from the sprawling suburbs of Los Angeles to the university archipelago of Cambridge, Massachussetts. Single men and women; married couples and children who have all but lost the finer nuances of their mother-tongue, are found in varying concentrations in the bigger metropolitan areas of the United States. Each one of them presents a unique set of problems which needs to be dealt with in a distinctly unAmerican way. Take the case of Dr Mashangu who while flying into Kennedy Airport on his first arrival in the United States broke down in tears when asked to furnish a permanent South African address on his entry papers. He had left South Africa in his thirties, yet by that time had not succeeded in convincing the South African authorites that he was entitled to a house to live in. It had been one of those cynical twists of fate which are as disabling as a congenital deformity, for Mashangu was the outcome of a joyous union of two black parents somewhere in a Northern Transvaal village. That tearfulness as he flew into Kennedy had been in store for him patiently like a long-awaited death. It was prime time for him to face the music.

Even in the United States with its motley of tribes, the refugee tends to stay afloat relentlessly trying to elude the melting pot. In the thriving refugee subcultures, refugees indulge in wild anniversary flings recreating social atmospheres whenever they can get together, if only to eat, drink and make love the way they know how.

It was Friday. Mashangu was expecting Mashela — a friend from New York City. He had served time on Robben Island before his mysterious escape from South Africa during the early sixties. When he phoned Mashangu early in the week, he literally bulldozed his way into an invitation to spend Friday evening in New Haven with him. Mashangu always lived beyond his means, saying philosophically that no black South African known to him could do otherwise and survive. As a visiting fellow teaching courses in Comparative Literature at an East Coast Ivy-League University, he still could not make ends meet. So, as he calculated the probable cost in dollars of the forthcoming evening, he could not help touching on certain questions surrounding his immediate future. His application for an immigrant visa was still with the American State Department. The South African authorities in New York City were sitting tight on his passport without letting him know whether it would be renewed or not. Neither was he assured of employment beyond the remaining eight months of his fellowship. In despair, he muttered to himself as he went out to buy provisions for the evening.

When Mashele and two black men, a white male and a young black woman arrived at Mashangu's apartment it was early evening. One of the black men Mashangu recognised immediately as Ngwenya, a frivolous Johannesburg attorney who was on a short visit to the country. Mashele shook hands with them, exchanging introductions where necessary as he went along. Ngwenya looked much older than when Mashangu had known him back home. The white man's name was Arya. He was a friend of Ngwenya's on a business trip abroad. A man in his thirties, he had a shag of hair about his head and face. The woman was introduced simply at Ntombi and none of her companions knew what she was doing in the States, except that she also had just arrived from the land of sunshine. She appeared like one of the new breed of black women who care a great deal about how their blackness comes through.

The initial social ineptness was absorbed in trivial conversation. The visitors settled down, sharing a peculiar distinctiveness. It was something which each one of them had to comprehend in a personal way. Small wonder that when these South Africans met at Mashangu's apartment the South African gloom gathered slowly around them. Like a bad dream, this darkness lurked behind them regardless of where they went.

They had been drinking and eating snacks for about two hours when a turn in the conversation occurred. Mashele

22

happened to say cynically: 'Hey chaps, imagine if we were back home in Soweto — say at Auntie Lizzie's maak uit? . . . what a fling whoring and drinking!'

'Whoring? . . . Why whoring?' insisted Ntombi.

'It's the people's idea of fun . . . nè boet Ngwenya?' Ntombi finished with eyes fixed on Ngwenya's face across the room.

Arya poured himself another stiff shot of scotch on the rocks. He was not going to be left out.

'What was that about whoring and fun?' he asked tersely. Ntombi gesticulated gracefully:

'I meant to say that there was a time when there were meaningful things for black people to do. People talked about the struggle, see? . . . They had a sense of participation. Involvement. After Sharpeville, their dream shrivelled up . . . died. What we have now is a nightmare.'

She stopped so suddenly that it was as if everything which needed to be said had been said. She mixed herself a dry martini and relaxed in her seat sipping it delicately.

'You are determined to spoil the evening. Aren't you?' snapped Ngwenya.

'No, boet Ngwenya,' retorted Ntombi impatiently.

'You are a good example, see. Successful types like you . . . tycoons . . . prefer amnesia.'

'Aha! here we go again. I've been wondering whether you people know what the hell you're talking about. Does it mean anything to you, Ntombi? Mark you, we don't know each other very well in this joint,' Mashele said, sinking back into his seat.

'Balls, I resent insinuations,' snapped Ntombi.

'You think we're softies, cowards, sell-outs. We've not been to the Island. Is that the idea?'

'Wait a minute,' interrupted Arya.

'Ntombi, you're blowing your cool on something Mashele didn't say. You're needling him, aren't you?'

'No deal! I know such types. It is the holier than thou attitude that blows my mind.'

Arya, playing mediator:

'You're coming out too strong, Ntombi.'

She was sitting next to him and appeared to enjoy being the only woman in the room. Changing the focus of her attack, she talked to Arya directly.

'I see . . . I would have been surprised. You mean to remain a charming white guest . . . no offence to your hosts, is that it? What a typical liberal, guilt-ridden and squirmish.'

'Come on Ntombi,' protested Arya in gentle tones.

'The question of white guilt interests me only in a personal way. That is, not as a collective issue and concern. How can I hope to make my interpretation of our situation at home acceptable to you? I don't stand a chance, do I? One way or other it will turn out to be arrogance or hypocrisy . . . You see I could not say I am with the black people in their plight without qualifying this statement. What if I said I didn't care a damn? Could I really say that and mean it?'

It was with a sense of secret amusement that Mashangu watched his guests begin to show signs of intoxication. When Mashangu emerged from his reverie to listen to the conversation again he heard Mashele proclaiming in a loud voice:

'It was at Varsity and later on the Island where I understood for the first time that the Euro-Africans are preoccupied with the creation of a mythological caucasion identity. None of that is peculiar to Southern Africa. It's an old disease . . . remember the Nazis? It's a matter of life and death — both physically and psychologically. Any group of settlers with a frontier outlook supported by conquest of the natives is obsessed with the development of an identity. To achieve that, mine had to be crushed out of existence.

'Let me add that there are no exceptions. Look at Arya here . . . He employs hundreds of blacks back home at starvation wages. That makes my blood boil. If I were man enough I should . . . History demands of us that we stretch ourselves out to the limit.'

There was a moment of silence. A kind of haze had settled over the entire apartment as though the conversation, alcohol fumes and tobacco smoke had joined hands in a malicious conspiracy. When nobody else spoke, Mashangu asked Arya what business he was in in South Africa.

'I am a publisher . . . You know the daily called *The People*?' replied Arya in a more relaxed tone.

'He's a pedlar of so-called Black News,' Mashele said caustically.

'Blacks make news don't they?' asked Arya in genuine surprise. He continued:

'At any rate, from a publisher's point of view they do.'

'Knock it off Arya, why can't you just say you are out for the buck, hé?' interposed Mashele as he poured himself a drink.

Ntombi was by now visibly drunk. She tottered to her feet, glass in hand and singing discordantly:

> *... Let's do it ... let's do it ...do it ... let's fall in love, even jelly-fish do it ... let's do it ... do it, Let's fall in love ...*

As she sang her way through the last words she flopped on Arya's lap. Suddenly she stopped singing and surveyed the room defiantly. In an equally defiant tone, she started to talk again:

'I say, how about some ... some dancing ... a little body heat, contact ... cheek to cheek like they do it in District Six ... what ... what is the point of talking about victims ... about murder when nobody is going to get killed? Suppose you Mashele ... should I say brother revolutionary? ... Suppose you had a few white victims with a sprinkling of so-called sell-outs like Ntombi ... you must be out of your minds ... Let's do it, let's fall in love ...'

Maybe they were out of their minds. They were all South African — one white surrounded by bitter natives thousands of miles from their own land. Each one of them had come on his or her own steam. Mashele had carved his way through East and West Africa, Europe and the Far East. The journey had nibbled away ten years of his youth and yet he was still on the run.

With Ntombi sitting on Arya's lap fondling him as she did, a new element was emerging in the situation. Arya became nervous under the vigilant eyes of the black men. Ntombi seemed intent on seducing them all simply by flirting with Arya.

'You're nervous, are you?' asked Ntombi reproachfully.

'No ... why? ... not in the least,' said Arya.

25

'How should I tell ... It's damn simple ... what I did. I moved over — sat on your lap and flung my lovely arms around your shoulders. You're a man, Arya. You must know the feeling ... vibrations.'

'Yes, but ...'

'Yes but what?' insisted Ntombi.

'How about a suggestion, in fact two suggestions?' Mashele inquired as though he were some kind of saviour.

'We could go out to a dig around town. Mashangu must know some hit joints around. Arya ... if you and Ntombi would prefer to stick together it's okay by me. We could pick you up on our way out you know.'

'I would really like some night-club experience,' said Arya hastily. 'It's a university town isn't it?'

'Be my guests,' Mashangu said and continued:

'If I had thought that would be your preference, we could have gone out earlier. This may well be prime time. Why don't we take a last round of drinks and go?'

The papering over the cracks had worked for the moment. The South Africans, one white, the others black, stumbled into the New England winter night the same way they stumble into each morning. They had no conscious knowledge of the outer limits of their anger, their frustrations, guilt, their hopes and their tolerance. They moved into their future the same way they invaded that night hardly knowing what joys or sorrows it would bring. The night embraced them all without reserve like the cold open thighs of a prostitute.

Go to Chapel Street if you wish on a Friday night and witness what Mashangu saw. They were all there — a mosaic of faces of men and women of letters wearing clothes that wobble and cling like half-formed fantasies. On Chapel Street Friday nights, one can buy pop-corn and brush oneself against a withering thigh. Other Friday sights befriend one on Chapel Street. An old woman grins for a smile as she crawls to her cell on Crown Street. On Chapel Street one may go to Robbin's Nest and see Nikki bubbling gum between sips and sighs.

As Mashangu walked into his apartment on 650 College Street, he could not escape the feeling of having gone through it all before. His visitors had left him to his solitary life at two o'clock in the morning. The apartment was a litter of glasses, bottles and cigarette stubs. Mashangu ignored the state of his apartment in favour of flopping on his bed to stare at the ceiling. He remembered Arya and soon his mind was whirling with ideas until he formulated the emerging sequence into the word 'arrogance'. Talking like one rehearsing for a play, he whispered to himself: 'You do not know what it is... arrogance ... till they define you as non-this or non-that. Till they sexualise your being and equate your body with excrement ... if that should leave you credulous ... if that should fail to destroy you ... if you should raise a finger ... wait till they tell you where you can go and how ... who you can marry and where ... where you can sleep, live and how ...' He fell asleep amid an excruciating protest.

Describing Okike to Chivuso, Mashangu had said that her body was like one enchanting terrain requiring a lifetime to explore. One man had apparently taken this fantasy for fact for he had decided to marry her in a hurry. He worked for the World Health Organisation, spending long spells of time in Africa and Europe. Okike, like most charming ladies who marry in a hurry, had been swallowed by her husband's enthusiasm, taking that to include everything which needed to be considered before a decision to marry is made.

The first time Mashangu met Okike he responded primarily to her outward sheen. She could be said to be self-conscious only in an extremely positive way. When she met Mashangu, she was living alone in a downtown apartment. Walking into the place, one could see her imprint all round. The arrangement of books, paintings, seating and standing space was sculptured to express an idea — that she the beautiful lady lived there. With her husband away most of the time, Okike still lived a full life. Occasionally she would go out with a friend. Most often she was content to be in her apartment writing, doing her university work or simply living.

Often, her heart would ache for her absent husband even though they often spoke to each other by phone across the seas. Until she met Mashangu, she had been very proud of what she jocularly described as her record. The trust and confidence her husband bestowed upon her had not been betrayed. Yet after Mashangu had called her, Okike immediately placed a call to her husband who was in Geneva at the time. This ploy had worked for it enabled her to sleep soundly until she woke up one night in the grip of an unusual dream. It had involved a man who though unknown to her had been very affectionate. To her horror, she had reciprocated without reservation.

In the days following the dream, she felt herself vulnerable. Full of anticipation of her dinner date with Mashangu, she elaborated several difficult situations in her fantasy in all of which she emerged unstained. She considered various practical ploys. She planned to introduce her husband's name into the conversation. If that should make Mashangu more insistent and jealous, she would bring her wedding rings into prominence. But as the day of the dinner approached, she wondered even more why she was unable to take this meeting with Mashangu for granted as she had done in other similar situations. Again she called her husband Friday night only to reproach herself afterwards for having been so silly.

Sunday came and Okike felt unprepared for it. Elaborate fantasies, hatched with meticulous care, vanished in the face of reality. As she lay in her comfortable bed at eleven in the morning she mused over this discovery. Competing with this realisation were various images of herself in several combinations of clothing. The phone started to ring. It was Mashangu on the line inquiring what she would like to eat and so on. Recoiling from an experience of full participation, she left all the decisions to him. Indeed, he made all the necessary decisions unaware of her motives in letting him shoulder the responsibility for both of them for the day.

For thirty minutes after talking to Mashangu she remained in bed. It felt safe in there. She raised herself finally, a mischevous smile lingering on her face. 'It is time to meet the faces that one knows,' she repeated as she hoisted herself out of bed. Stretching every muscle of her body, she watched her reflection in a full-size mirror and marvelled at it all. There were a few routine things to be done before Mashangu came for her at three that afternoon.

She prepared a simple breakfast consisting of coffee, orange juice, an egg and a slice of toasted bread. The beast is being fattened for the feast, she reflected with amusement at her sensuous imagery. Okike believed that dressing up was, for a woman, a moment of real creativity. The outcome had to say something about her. Once she had finished breakfast she went about creating, sculpturing an image of herself which she wanted to bring forth and took her time doing it.

As the time of Mashangu's arrival approached, Okike felt more ready and relaxed. Her sense of mastery and level of comfort surprised her. She was full of anticipation steeped in the sensations and images of her dream. The strange man appeared to her imagination vividly again — his darting eyes and herself lying on the bed coy but satiated. Unmindful of the time, she was startled from this reverie by the ringing of the door-bell. She stood up from where she had been sitting on a recliner and walked straight to the door to let Mashangu in.

They exchanged fleeting glances as Okike invited Mashangu into the livng room.

'Well, I haven't been outside this apartment since last night. How is it out there?' inquired Okike.

'It is rather seasonal . . . but a little on the warm side. You'll probably need a coat though.'

'Well then, excuse me for a second,' Okike said, moving towards the bedroom. Her brief absence gave Mashangu a chance to familiarise himself with his immediate surroundings. There was much to see in the room but Mashangu decided that Okike was so much more interesting than the room.

Okike was dressed in an ankle-length floral dress. It obscured her shapely legs but not her body configuration. Her bustline was prominently anchored below a lively face topped with well groomed pitch-black hair. She reappeared from the bed-room and Mashangu stood up to join her.

When Mashangu and Okike left the apartment, they drove in Mashangu's car to a Chinese restaurant a few miles away from the downtown area. Mashangu had had dinner there once before with some student friends and had liked the food and service. By the time they arrived at Chinese Gardens, it was early evening. The winter darkness was beginning to settle over the ridges of the hills and highrise apartment buildings. They started their dinner with cocktails and took their time deciding what to order, talking as a kind of foreplay before the upsurge of consuming appetites. The setting was ideal for such a climax. The lighting, soft music in the background and the humming and whispers of those around them created an erotic and exotic atmosphere which could not fail to infuse itself into their feeling and conversation. They talked about neutral subjects, as if to obscure the surging emotions which served as an undercurrent to their conversation and appetites.

Okike made passing references to her marital status at two or three points during their conversation, but that was not enough to detract Mashangu from his firm resoluteness. He was sifting his own feelings as they bubbled over into every movement and the words he uttered knowing full well that he could not feel that way unless Okike was reciprocating. Indeed she was, only with a delicacy of gesture and tone of voice that conveyed a very physical nature. She could bring herself out through the sheer synchronicity of her body and refined sensibility. To Mashangu she appeared as an invitation to a nakedness of spirit. She seemed like something which apart from a certain youthful courage expressed trust in the benevolence of the universe. It was this experience at dinner which nourished Mashangu's courage to new levels of intensity as the evening glided by.

Once they had gone through the main course, they decided on coffee. Coffee drinking ushered a new feel of intimacy between them as they ventured away from neutral subjects of conversation. 'You probably wondered why I dared to call you so late that night after we had had dinner with Chivuso,' started Mashangu retrospectively. 'Well, I just thought you were some kind of romantic. Besides, it is not that unusual for the phone to ring at that time of morning. Sometime as you pick it up to respond, the other party hangs up.

'I felt I could not wait another day unless I had managed to establish some continuing contact with you. I know women often take that kind of feeling for a male fiction. For me it was a very neat impulse. I wanted to acknowledge both to myself and you that you had made a strong impression on me . . . I wanted to acknowledge that I had felt ecstatic and wanted to be able to share that with you . . . I meant everything I said to you that night. Even as I sit here, nothing has changed.' As Mashangu said the last words his eyes which had been roaming over Okike's face and bust glanced for a moment at the table. There was her beautiful hand with long strong fingers that carried the ceremonial rings glittering in the dim light. Okike realized that Mashangu was regarding her hand. She wanted to withdraw it but it was too late. Mashangu was fingering it with a caress that could be seen in his eyes.

'Don't you think we should be on our way?' inquired Okike. 'Okay,' replied Mashangu releasing Okike's hand. 'Maybe I should say this right away. Both of us have histories you see . . . commitments to others . . . that is something around our necks maybe for a lifetime. But . . . the only freedom that remains as everything else crumbles around us is a small island big enough for two . . . The primal myth of the Garden of Eden is necessary in this century more than ever before.' Mashangu was interrupted by the waitress who brought the change. They left a tip on the table and started out on their way back to the city.

The word love was not mentioned even in their most intimate conversation that day. There were moments of exhilarating closeness checked now and again by considerations of propriety. When they said farewell to each other at Okike's apartment it was with a mutual feeling that in spite of all the difficulties in their way it could not be the end. Something had been released and set in motion that required the best in each one of them to contain. Okike retreated into her little island to console herself with the thought that she had only responded as naturally as she had felt at the time. At no time had she said 'yes' to anything that Mashangu had said to her. That should suffice, she thought to herself, even though the world could reproach her for having desisted from saying 'no, it can't be so.' 'Why don't I feel guilty?' she murmured to herself. 'Why should I feel guilty for being myself . . . what is there to be guilty about anyway?' she finished as she took off her shoes.

My toes . . . my nails . . . my body . . . me. At high school back home . . . that abominable school teacher called me the African queen . . . the serpent of the Nile . . . I was a virgin then ... bursting at the seams. Then came Kofi ... he seemed all innocence ... like I was ... it was a Sunday evening I remember ... behind the church yard ... I could have screamed. Thank God my husband doesn't know who started the journey of discovery ... what a euphemism for a simple matter! Then there was Richard in France ... the mother ... he could only ... some people are like that. Maybe Mashangu ... so sensitive ... maybe everything is coiled up in his head. Damn! What a thought! ... the seminar tomorrow on the World versus South Africa in the case of the people of Namibia ... I should have discussed it with Mashangu ... Aha! ... I will call his apartment, no. Yes, I will ... let him fret about my motives ... I will call him ... business, business like. Okike took off her clothing, one item at a time until she was confronted with her own nakedness. Good thing Mashangu did not try anything funny ... I am so high strung ... waited, waiting for that man in Geneva ... spend Christmas in Austria ... Vienna. My dear hubby ... wonder who he has kissed ... is kissing ... good idea to interrupt him in the act ... in the best of things ... his phone will ring. 'Wait a minute,' he'll say. 'It must be Okike ... she usually calls this time ... I won't be a minute. Damn, let it ring, I'll call her tomorrow ...' A shower would do me some good. Maybe a little preparation for tomorrow's seminar. Okike stood up from the bedside chair on which she had been sitting. Moving slowly towards the bathroom, she heard the phone ring. Take it right here ... in the bedroom ... eleven thirty ... it may be Ike. Could it be Mashangu? Better to find out. 'Hi,' said Okike as she picked up the receiver.

'Well, what do you know, I thought of calling you about something ... glad you called first,' said Okike. 'It's about some questions I have about the Namibia question ... No. Something about the domestic reaction to the last World Court judgement and subsequent United Nations resolutions and actions ... Yes, yes, that is right. I see ... I see ... that's right. ... Well, what time is your talk? Eight in the evening? ... I see ... A memorial lecture, how distinguished ... You don't make much of it ... I think it can be arranged ... Have dinner before the lecture? ... It seems too soon to ... to do it

32

again. . . . Are you sure that's how you feel? . . . I'll call you tomorrow at your office . . . you may be out of luck . . . I'll think about it. The lecture is okay though . . . I don't know about dinner.' Neither of them seemed to want the conversation to come to an end but it trailed off into farewell sighs and hisses.

Although Mashangu had not said much about the Alfred Elliot Memorial lecture to his friends and students, he had been preparing for it over a period of time. When he was invited by the university to give the lecture, he accepted readily, feeling that it was a serious responsibility which he felt capable of shouldering. The important thing, he had reflected at the time, was to find a theme close to both his experience and his literary interests. It had been with a sense of gathering excitement that Mashangu presented the topic of his lecture to the dean of the school of Arts and Sciences. 'Incident at Vichy: A tribute to the Sociological Imagination' was as exciting a theme as anyone could wish to present for a memorial lecture in the humanities.

Mashangu spent most of Monday putting the finishing touches to his lecture. Only occasionally did he think of other matters such as when Okike had called him. They had spoken for about fifteen minutes on the phone and had sealed the whole affair with a decision to go to dinner together before going to the lecture. Okike had agreed, feeling for her own part that maybe Mashangu needed some support. Little did she know that her intuition was leading her on to something beyond the memorial lecture. She expected to detect signs of anxiety or nervousness in Mashangu. Either he was too good at dissembling or there were just none that she could feel. They had dinner at one of the university halls where apart from a little chit chat here and there with people known to either of them, they awaited the decisive moment during which Mashangu would spread himself out.

After dinner, they took a slow walk to Bradley Hall. Already at that time scores of people could be seen gathering at the entrance to the hall. Mashangu had listened to several lectures at Bradley Hall before. In the audience . . . the audience. Okike will be in the audience . . . up front. Chivuso too . . . he promised to come ... the chairman of the department ... his wife Helen ... cluttered with jewellery. All these people, several hundreds ... sitting ... changing seats, whispering, believe in the dean ... the committee ... no, they believe in me ... believe I have something to say. A foreign scholar ... Ladies and gentlemen ... the chair will say: 'Mashangu is a distinguished visiting fellow in comparative literature ...' the usual rhetoric will follow. Distinguished my foot! The honourable dean should add: ignored in his native country ... now he finds he is without a job in this ... Mashangu had to part company with Okike. She chose a seat along the second row from the front. Mashangu exchanged a few words with Professor Todd who was in the chair as silence began to descend over the whispers and shuffles in the auditorium.

'Ladies and gentlemen.' started Professor Todd in a loud voice. 'Today I have the honour to present to you visiting Professor Mashangu whose distinguished career is known to the university community and is clearly reflected in the biographical sketch currently in your possession. The Alfred Elliot Memorial lecture is held once each year to enable this university and scholars the world over to pay tribute to a man who in his short life made one of the most significant contributions to humanistic culture.' He moved from the rostrum as he finished to vacate the stand for Mashangu. As Mashangu stood up to move to the rostrum, there was a resounding clapping of hands.

'Ladies and gentlemen, I wish to thank the university for thinking me worthy of this honour. The theme of my address is the sociological imagination as we encounter it in all great literature. More specifically, I would like to pay tribute tonight to this quality of mind, this sensibility as we find it in Miller's *Incident at Vichy*. Let me begin by quoting C. Wright Mills, the sociologist, who once wrote: "In the absence of an adequate social science, critics and novelists, dramatists and poets have been the major, and often the only, formulators of private troubles and even public issues."

'Apart from the fact that Miller's *Incident at Vichy* is such an important enrichment to humanistic culture it unfolds itself to me as a work of art in which we are privileged to witness the fruits of the sociological imagination. It represents the highest possible integration in the creative act of personal tragedy with public issues. We find dramatised in it the moment of intersection between biography and history.

'Personal troubles inhabit the character structure of an individual and his experience — the personal idiomatic sphere. On the other hand, an issue is a public matter often involving institutional alignments and oppositions. One thing seems clear, ladies and gentlemen, and it is that in making a distinction between troubles and issues we are dealing with a differential expressivity of reality. At best the mature intelligence like Miller's concerns itself with the interface between personal troubles and public issues.

'Ladies and gentlemen, in paying tribute to Miller, I also want to emphasise that in *Incident at Vichy,* he brings us face to face with the irrational, the absurd and even more importantly, the incomprehensible. Miller the artist feels at home in telling us that a condition in life is incomprehensible — that it is possible to be shamelessly ignorant about life.

'Early in the drama, the following exchange occurs between Bayard (an electrician) and Lebeau the painter:

Bayard — 'Yes, but it's not all that simple. You should try to think of why things happen. It helps to know the meaning of one's suffering.'

Lebeau replies a few lines later:

'Well I'm not a philosopher, but I know my mother, and that's why I'm here. You're like people who look at my paintings — "What does this mean, what does that mean?" Look at it, don't ask what it means; you are not God, you can't tell what anything means. I'm walking down the street before a car pulls up beside me, a man gets out and measures my nose, my ears, my mouth, the next thing I'm sitting in a police station — or whatever the hell this is here — and in the middle of Europe, the highest peak of civilisation! And you know what it means? After the Romans and the Greeks and the Renaissance, and you know what this means?'

'Ladies and gentlemen, the poignancy of Lebeau's questions is heightened by the total context of the drama. Although everything in the setting has a fairy tale quality about it, there are excruciating realities to be faced by the participants. In historically extreme situations, even law and order assume the formlessness of vulgarity to such an extent that it is no longer possible to disentagle ends from means. In *Incident at Vichy,* Lebeau and others keep wondering whether the building in which they are detained is indeed a prison. The charges against them are equally unclear to the extent that Lebeau with characteristic restlessness of spirit is forced to ask:

'This isn't a prison, is it?'

'Then:

'You begin wishing you'd committed a crime, you know? Something definite.'

'But in the unfolding of the drama, it becomes clear that in the conditions of contemporary life it is no longer necessary to commit a definite and unquestionable crime to be judged guilty or experience guilt. To commit a live, real crime, one would have to be an individual in his or her own right. In a world in which nothing is forbidden, what remains is an illusion of participation in the destiny of societies. Leduc pronounces the ultimate judgement:

'Until you know it is true of you you will destroy whatever truth can come of this atrocity. Part of knowing who we are is knowing we are not someone else. And Jew is only the name we give to that stranger, that agony we cannot feel, that death we look at like a cold abstraction. Each man has his jew; it is the other. And the Jews have their Jews. And now above all, you must see that you have yours — the man whose death leaves you relieved that you are not him, despite your decency. And that is why there is nothing and will be nothing — until you face your own complicity with this . . . your own complicity.'

'In the historically extreme situation, ladies and gentlemen, we have total complicity in which everyone is guilty. At the end of Miller's drama there is still nothing. The reader is not gratified by an over-riding understanding of the historically extreme situation, least of all by a possibility for corrective action. In the end like in the beginning, all that is available to a man and his jew or Nigger, the racist and his victim, is a turbulent silence, a chance to stare into each other's eyes! Racism, wherever and whenever it is operative, is a public issue. Yet it is also true that in the lives of millions of individuals it assumes the form of a personal trouble.

'It is the personal troubles, the individual destinies, that add a dimension to the problem of the historically extreme situation in *Incident at Vichy*. Here one can think of the businessman and his sleek ways; the boy and his desperate concern for his mother and the old jew who stuck to his bag of feathers. All these characters have to be seen within the context of a public historical issue: the fact that somebody with power and authority had decreed that Jews could be exterminated.

'Ladies and gentlemen, let me say that with Miller's sociological imagination at work, a human concern which is both personal and public, biographical and historical, is fused in the dramatic moment. Incident at Vichy is a wide, limitless canvas and we should really be remorseful since we are bound to share the hubris, the vulgarity and the burden of ignorance crystallised in the dramatic moment. What could be more unpromising than Miller's depiction of the Major and Von Berg at the close of the drama: "They stand there, forever incomprehensible to one another, looking into each other's eyes." '

The lecture in its entirety took about an hour and fifteen minutes. Mashangu spoke with unnerving conviction from beginning to end, only looking at his notes from time to time when it was necessary to quote something or other. He could tell by the end of his lecture that he had had a good reception. Several people from the audience came forward at the end of his talk to congratulate him.

'Brilliant,' observed Okike as she joined Mashangu at the door to walk to the car. 'Thank you,' replied Mashangu with a broad smile on his face. 'There is one thing though,' continued Mashangu. 'I would have liked it better if there had been an opportunity for an exchange of views. That is what I enjoy most in seminars and symposia. Shall we have coffee or a drink and talk a little before I take you home? We could drive over to my place.' Without thinking about it, Mashangu was holding Okike's hand and had suddenly come to a standstill. Okike looked up into his eyes and said teasingly:

'You never give up do you? How about some other time?'

'I see. You are like the shrew, you need taming, right?' insisted Mashangu coaxingly.

'Come on,' responded Okike with mock seriousness. 'It's just that you come on like a tornado . . . one needs time . . . time to sort things out.' She gave him another searching look and he rewarded her with a firm squeeze of her hand. They started to walk again until they reached the car. As they settled into their respective seats Mashangu started to talk again:

'Well, yesterday you let me decide where we should go out to eat. I will indulge myself one more time, okay?' Okike did not reply. She merely looked at him in a manner which suggested compliance. They drove in relative silence until they reached Mashangu's apartment.

'What will it be, coffee or a drink? Let me see what I have. I have some beer, a little scotch and some vodka. I'll fix myself some scotch.'

Okike was undecided for a moment. 'Scotch with some ice,' she said finally.

Mashangu moved into the kitchen to mix the drinks. What a woman! he thought as he took out the glasses. Lips that are full like ripe black berries. Sensuous movements her hips make . . . some other time. That's what she'll say. Not so soon . . . we don't know each other very well . . . I bet that's what you say, do to other women . . . nothing special . . . the men in her life. There must have been many. Is that a bad thing in itself? . . . yes and no. He returned to the room with two glasses, some cheese, cold meats and exotic looking nuts on a tray. He offered Okike her glass and stood there regarding her whole being with relish. With a muffled sigh he sat beside her on the sofa so closely that he could feel the contours of her body shifting a little out of reach.

'Don't you tire of looking at me the way you do?' asked Okike.

'Has anybody ever told you they did?' asked Mashangu in return.

'Well, when I was an adolescent, I was all a chunk of fat, you know. My mother used to tell me she couldn't stand the sight of me. She was not malicious, of course . . . just a manner of talking. People look at others for all kinds of reasons . . .

Americans resent being stared at as you probably know. I don't mind really.'

'It's difficult to describe what I was feeling when I was looking at you,' said Mashangu with enough feeling to escape into the tone of his voice. 'I seem to trust you to know what I am feeling without even as much as saying a word about it. Isn't that strange? I imagine that is how the infant experiences its trust of its universe before it bruises itself.'

'Come on little boy, stop teasing,' said Okike after a hearty laugh.

'I am serious,' Mashangu said as he prepared himself for a long sip of scotch. 'Doesn't it mean anything to you what I feel?' he inquired affectionately.

'You are not expecting an answer are you?' retorted Okike. She continued: 'You must realise that it is women who carry the burden of morality . . . I am a married woman . . . I need not have even said that damn me, but I have to think of every little move I make. A woman is always looking at the mirror wherever she goes . . . she sees herself reflected in the social opinion of her as person . . . as woman. Supposing I indulged my own nature, my own spontaneity with you, you could use it against me . . . You could call me names and what is worse even lose whatever interest you may have had. Right?'

'What you say is true only in a general way,' Mashangu said. 'You are talking about cold abstractions . . . marriage . . . morality. I am saying: here is this exquisite woman whose warmth I feel radiating through my innermost being . . . the power of a virile gentleness.' With his right hand on Okike's lap, Mashangu started to stroke her thigh gently. Okike held his hand in mild protest as she said: 'Tell me about the women in your life.'

'Let me get us another drink first,' Mashangu said standing to go to the kitchen.

The women in my life! Who? When? Where? I remember Nomsa. We exploded the silence of our youth and bodies together . . . after several nights of struggle something broke . . . celebrated the initiation with sound sleep. Both virgins . . . what do they call the youthful man whose body is still silent? No matter. Many years later . . . Dorothy whose

39

father let all hell loose after a successful abortion. He was after my balls ... I could not help his sense of moral outrage. The rest of the women ... their names and faces vanished with the darkness ... sighs and drunken noises. Mashangu returned with the drinks.

'You were asking about the women in my life,' Mashangu said as he flopped on the seat close to Okike. He looked her straight in the eyes and said: 'You really want to know? The first lady was Sophia ... my mother. I had her all to myself for several years. The old fellow used to come once a year from Johannesburg. The poor fellow was making the masters rich. He lived for a while with a Zulu woman ... a third mother I never met in Johannesburg.'

'Small wonder you are so spoiled ... You are used to having your whim all the time. Aren't you, little man?' Okike said teasingly.

'I sure enjoy being spoiled by you,' Mashangu said putting his arm around Okike's waist. He continued: 'If I let you in on a secret ... if I should say I have always been a cynic as far as women go ... that I've just forgotten, forgotten a great many of them without as much as a question, how many points do I lose or gain in your estimation?'

'None in any direction,' was Okike's quick reply.

'Maybe I should add that I've always anticipated a whirlwind of a romance with a somewhat exotic woman. What do you know? When I found her, she was all married. She is sitting right here. All that remains is animated fantasy about us ... not now but in the future.' His facial expression had become more serious. Okike noticed the change, shifted about on the seat, thought of going away to her apartment but said nothing about it.

Mashangu removed his arm from Okike's waist in one quick movement. He took her hand from her lap, clasping it firmly to move it to a position between his thighs. 'Stop it, you little devil,' said Okike in seductive mockery.

'Just a little tenderness will do,' said Mashangu, snuggling up to Okike expectantly.

Monday night had been a short night. Now it was Tuesday

morning and Mashangu remained in bed for about an hour going over Monday night. The Memorial lecture . . . something students will talk about for the rest of the week . . . really unimportant. Okike . . . she lay here last night, this morning . . . at my side . . . below . . . together . . . warm. All that protest . . . consideration for others, foreplay. There I go again . . . an . . . at six in the morning! I love her . . . she does. Words no, talking about it will destroy. Talk about other things, people, politics, science, philosophy and art. Words, symbols: charming. I am not Romeo: 'this is the East and Juliet is the sun.' Nor Ernobabus: 'Age could not wither her nor custom stale her infinite variety.' . . . Action . . . praxis . . . movement, pulse, sensation . . . the body in rapture. The legacy of whole civilisations . . . . . . more words and symbols. Time to wake up . . . quick shower . . . no breakfast. Coffee. The Shrink . . . this afternoon at four . . . I've changed my mind. Will call Okike this evening.

Until Mashangu went to check his mail, there had been nothing unusual that Tuesday. There were several letters which he glanced at quickly as he walked briskly to his office. One letter attracted his attention because it had the emblem of the South African Embassy in Washington. He put the rest of the letters on his desk and said loudly: 'Damn them, what is it this time?' He tore the envelope open to pull out the letter which he began to read closely:

Dear Dr Mashangu
Your application for an extension and renewal of your South African passport has been receiving active consideration. I hope that you will appreciate our desire to proceed with considerable care in considering such requests. After conducting routine investigations, the Honourable Dr Adendorff has determined that you should report to our Consular offices in New York on November 18 at 2 p.m. It is always the firm policy of this Mission and my government to be firm but just in our dealing with our citizens at home and abroad.
Sincerely
JAN POTGIETER
First Secretary.

Dr Adendoff, Jan Potgieter ... 'firm but just' ... 'Routine investigations' ... they told me that, many times, in Pretoria when I applied for a passport several months ... routine investigations. It's meant to break me down ... it was before and is now. My mind, my imagination ... my fantasy must do the job for them ... imagine the routine investigations ... how they will check everything ... Everything. Some uncouth nondescript will present it to me ... will pace up and down the room: 'the law has a long arm' ... 'It is always the firm policy' ... consistency ... law and order, democracy, rule of law, civilisation. I must be broken down ... my own mind must do the job. I must believe that and be a *goeie Kaffer*. Smart, 'I am to go for an interrogation in New York City, November 18. No. That is not true ... I am always under interrogation. Have to prove something ... nothing because nobody knows what I should prove. 'Do you really mean what you say ... do you really love me?' Cocktail party talk ... The The Cocktail Party, T. S. Eliot ... The Wasteland ... living in rats' alley at the beginning of this century already ... T. S. Eliot saw it all ... life in this century is a cigarette stub in a London Street gutter. We live in rats' alley ... Now is the time to take up arms ... I will reward him and his kin with a full presence. I am not ... I am not crazy. I see it clearly now, I am not neurotic and will tell Davies that much. Right to his face!

Mashangu banged a clenched fist on the desk as he stood up to leave his office. He left the rest of the mail untouched for the day. At seminars and other meetings that day several people wondered why he looked so withdrawn, preoccupied. He merely shrugged his shoulders to the mumble of a quick succession of words which left his interlocuters even more surprised. In more formal situations he presented a calm thoughtfulness which masked a more flamboyant disposition.

It was in such a state of mind that Mashangu walked into Dr Davies' office at four o'clock. He flopped into the nearest seat in a manner which felt defiant to him. He checked himself as he reminded himself that Davies was not Potgieter or Retief but an American. If there was a difference between Davies and Potgieter, it was too subtle for Mashangu to experience and see at the time. He waited in vain for a provocation, even a slight

42

one, such as a cough or a change of facial expression on Davies' part. Davies sat and waited.

'I didn't think it would happen so soon,' Mashangu said as if he were dragging the words out. 'I have made up my mind . . . I also think it is the right decision . . . don't try to persuade me otherwise.' Mashangu took out a cigarette and lit it silently. Davies could feel the anger and urgency in Mashangu's tone of voice but was at a loss about where it came from or was leading to. Davies said: 'You are upset about some decision you've made. It would help if you could say more about it.'

'What is the use of sitting here trying to share my unhappiness with you when in a general sense you may be part of my problem?' asked Mashangu, gesticulating freely.

'I cannot deny you your feelings but I do think that it may be helpful to explore the matter further,' said Davies with evident self-possession.

'It is clear to me that you are a well-meaning person in your own way,' Mashangu said a little more calmly. 'It won't do any harm to be open with you. Something happened today . . . a kind of culmination in a long array of insults which have been heaped on me since I was born. I know . . . It is clear from the letter I received from the South African Embassy that they are withdrawing my passport. They will not renew it. They are kind of setting me afloat as a citizen of no country as though everything they've done so far were not enough.'

'I can appreciate how indignant you must feel. Was this outcome unexpected?' asked Davies.

'Nobody gets used to neo-barbarism of this kind. It's a fresh wound each time even before the others have had a chance to heal. When I left South Africa, I was holding on tight-fistedly to compassion and tolerance. I used to think that it was always possible for humanism to triumph over tyranny; they have incubated the beast in me to maturity . . . to go out into the jungle in search of other beasts.'

'I respect your feeling of utter indignation,' Davies said, 'yet you've not yet talked much about the decision.'

'It's two decisions in one. The beast is come into the open and you don't have to know what that is about. That's for me and my oppressors. What does concern you is that the first decision

43

also means that I am clearing the hell out of therapy,' Mashangu felt arrogant in therapy for the first time.

'Please tell me how the second decision follows from the first,' Davies said without any indication of surprise.

'From what I can make out you are not a Jew,' started Mashangu arrogantly. 'You are simply Caucasian, WASP . . . There is no need for you to accept what I am about to say. I'll say it all the same. You and your society have exhausted the revolutionary possibilities of your life . . . I don't know offhand how all this fits in, but you are vulnerable to neurotic and metaphysical anxiety. What I've come to know is that my own revolutionary possibilities, those of my people, are at their highest at this point . . . I am suffering as I do and have done . . . not from neurosis, metaphysical anxiety, but from a negation of the rebellious impulse in me. What I need is not analysis . . . the verbal and symbolic realm. Action . . . I need to do things. It's not inside this skull that work needs to be done but out there in the realm of social and historical action'. Mashangu took out a cigar that a friend had offered him earlier and moved it about his fingers, feeling its roundness and texture. He lit it in angry contemplation.

'As your therapist, my first inclination is to want to be as helpful as I can. Given the circumstances, it is not clear to me how best I can achieve such a result. However, it seems to me that you feel continuing in therapy would not only be a waste of time but that it is something antithetical to your current plans,' Davies said raising his eyebrows and fingering the bowl of his pipe.

'Indeed!' Mashangu said with his whole frame. 'You will never know what I've had to go through to maintain some semblance of sanity . . . what my people have to go through in the land of their birth . . . Their own land, mind you. There is one thing . . . one thing.' Mashangu continued, his voice beginning to falter. He could feel that his eyes were becoming watery and tried fervently to remain self-possessed merely by concentrating on what he was saying.

'There is one thing,' Mashangu said with more concerted effort this time: 'I remember when I arrived in this country . . . the first few months were a brutal nightmare. I was so enraged, agitated, almost always in a shiver. For a while I was perplexed until I had a murderous fantasy which I wrote about the other day. It hits you in the face, consumes you like a frenzy ... the day you make the radical discovery that there is a killer stirring within you demanding recognition. Then you fan yourself into murderous rage when you say to yourself: 'That white man who insulted me in the street ... that one who beat up my friend on the highway, those others who showered bullets into my people, that history Professor with his racist obsenities and the ones at the Pass Office, the Passport Office: I should have ...!' Mashangu thumped the armrest of the chair he was sitting on with a clenched fist as if to articulate each sentence more forcefully.

Davies kept his gaze on Mashangu and said: 'You feel no inclination at this point to explore the extent of your rage by remaining in therapy for some time.'

Mashangu did not respond immediately. He remained silent for a moment, suppressing an impulse to stand up and pace up and down the office. He considered a walkout but restrained himself, electing to see the interview to its finish.

Mashangu said: 'Don't you see the utter futility of talking about my rage ?... Words, words and symbols ... impotent rage, that's what it becomes when one elects to think and talk about it. You see it in this country, the substitution of indignation with words and symbols. You walk into the streets and see the black male who substitutes his rage for a brief encounter with a white prostitute, soaking himself wet to the beat of soul. It's the same in South Africa, only there are no white tramps to abuse because of the Immorality Act. All these men felt the beast stirring within at one time or another ... the murderous impulse.

'Everybody, friends, wives and even therapists told them it was bad to feel that way ... words and symbols actively came into play. "Watch out: the system will kill you" people say and the murderous impulse is transformed into a sexual perversion of one kind or another. You know what I mean ... Look at my black brothers in Harlem or anywhere in this country for that matter. It's as if they were saying: "I can't beat him at the stock exchange and the Pentagon ... Congress? No! ... I'll hit below the belt — at a most primitive level — and will make him choke with anger." I am afraid that's not the African solution ... my solution. There must be other alternatives. Something more creative ... less primitive than a sexual offensive. I'm quitting therapy to-day and that is final.'

Davies shifted in his chair as he started to talk. 'I can appreciate how you must feel even as I believe that you should have availed yourself of the opportunity of analysing your experience of outrage instead of acting it out in one form or another. Your decision is fully respected, of course. Allow me to add that should you feel like talking things over again, you should not hesitate to call and make an appointment.'

Mashangu expressed his appreciation of the offer. Although the two men managed to talk for about twenty minutes longer no change in their arrangements occurred. By the time Mashangu left Dr Davies' office the tension had lessened somewhat.

When Mashangu left the clinic, he went straight to his apartment. As he walked into the elevator, he was greeted by a charming young white woman who lived on the sixth floor. Mashangu had exchanged greetings with her before noticing only peripherally that she was beautiful. On this day, however, Mashangu had experienced something new in responding to her greeting and coyish smile. He returned her greeting and smiled warmly as he took her in from head to toe with his penetrating eyes. In return, she sprawled out another coy smile as Mashangu bade her farewell on leaving the elevator. Fumbling for keys in his pockets as he went along the corridor, he thought to himself: impotent rage ... that's what I told Davies. It's true ... nothing erotic about it. Nothing ... I should know about that. I told Davies so, hardly an hour ago ... Black men and white women washing down anger with semen ... putting it away in oohs and aahs ... Victims of symbols ... we all are.

He opened the door and felt the warmth in the room radiating through his body. Supper ... A quick supper, then a few important phone calls to make ... trifling little things like a radiant smile ... a spirited embrace that leaves one panting or an infant enwombed in mother's arms ... little things help us navigate through the mirage. This life . . . as though there were any other, thought Mashangu as he sat on the bed to take off his shoes. The artist Mashangu must leave the realm of symbols, words, to create in action in the jungle. I said to Davies: 'a singleness of purpose' . . . 'the path of the sword.'

The phone started ringing. Mashangu stood up to answer it. 'How are you?' he responded animatedly. It was Okike. 'I am glad you called . . .' Mashangu said. 'When? . . . THIS EVENING? . . . who are they? . . . Dr and Mrs Skelton . . . I see . . . both doctors at the Yale-New Haven Hospital . . . splendid . . . I was just thinking about what to have for dinner . . . the prospect of seeing you sooner . . . Your car . . . Okay I'll be right over at seven, right? Lots of love and so long.'

After his telephone conversation with Okike, Mashangu had a bath. The phone call to Mashele in New York was postponed for later that night. At six-thirty he was ready to move out to Okike's apartment where he was to join her for the drive to the Skeltons. Mashangu, a devout believer in informal dress, contented himself with grey pants topped with a grey polo neck jersey under a black leather jacket for the evening. He did not entertain himself with the prospect of dinner with the Skeltons. Uppermost in his mind was Okike — the calm after a stormy day.

On arrival at Okike's apartment, he parked the car hastily and literally ran up the stairs to her door. She was ready and waiting. Mashangu flung his arms around her neck, giving her little time for any trivial formalities. Pulling herself away gently and leading Mashangu to a seat Okike said: 'Listen, steady now . . . I won't be a second. Give me a chance to get the car keys in the bedroom.'

'Am I welcome there too?' asked Mashangu teasingly.

'You are not on heat are you?' retorted Okike, disappearing into the bedroom.

As Okike reappeared in the living room, Mashangu stood up and said: 'The Skeltons, what kind of folks are they . . . friends of yours eh?'

'Sort of.' responded Okike, giggling. 'One of these experimental unions,' Okike said tapping Mashangu's shoulder.

'Experimental union? . . . odious isn't it?'

They walked down the stairs to the first landing. As they entered the car, Okike continued: 'It's a mixed couple. I don't want to alarm you in any way but . . . they are funnier than the odd couple. Stella is a black American. She grew up in Harlem, studied in England for a while. I believe that's where she met Jack. I imagine they fell in love and a week therafter they were man and wife.'

'How romantic,' Mashangu said as he sagged back into his seat.

'You needn't be cynical . . . it's entirely possible that . . . snapped Okike looking at Mashangu's reaction out of the corner of her eye. She noted a change in his facial expression and decided to talk about something neutral.

'Have you ever been to Guildford?'

'Guildford, no' answered Mashangu.

'Well, continued Okike, 'we'll turn into I 95, Connecticut turnpike North until we get to Exit 58. In the Spring it's simply gorgeous. Now it's all snow in the countryside. I met the Skeltons last summer at a party at Professor Smeltzer's joint. They invited me to go horse riding. Did you know I ride horses? Well, I never told you . . . the Skeltons have two Arabian horses. Cute isn't it? Watch out for the exit. We shouldn't end up in Boston on a chit chat spree.'

'It's going to be the fifth from here,' Mashangu said, thumbing Okike along her right thigh.

'You haven't told me what you've been doing since I last saw you,' Okike said inquiringly.

'Rotten day,' Mashangu said.

'Come on, tell me about it. It seems to have upset you,' Okike said, sounding concerned.

'Later, not now. That might spoil our evening with the medicos, see.'

In the silence which followed Mashangu's remark, they travelled another three miles off the Inter-State Highway into Guildford proper. Most of the area, apart from driveways, was still snow-covered. Along the road could be seen a mass of white undulating up and down the hills with lights from homesteads twinkling at uneven intervals. The Skeltons lived in East-coast, almost old New England style in an eleven-roomed country house complete with stables and sprawling lawns. Imposing as the house was from outside, it was modestly furnished, showing in a way like nothing else in the neighbourhood that the inhabitants were professional and academic people.

Okike and Mashangu were met at the door by Stella who greeted Okike warmly and said. 'Oh my Okike, what a find! Who's the brother . . . from Africa, isn't he?'

Okike was quick to respond to save Mashangu some embarrassment. She said: 'Mashangu, meet Stella . . . the hostess.'

'Pleased to meet you,' said Mashangu, shaking Stella's hand.

Stella invited them upstairs to meet the folk, requesting them to please take off their shoes, adding: 'You will not believe this but it's true, we make love upstairs. On the floor see? Kind of weird. Come along.' After they had taken off their coats and shoes the three hopped up the stairs to the second level into a large living room with a fire crackling from a fireplace.

'Jack, meet Mashangu. Of course you know Okike,' Stella started with the introductions.

'Hi, nice to meet you and welcome,' responded Jack in a thick, almost Bostonian accent. He was a tall bearded man of about thirty-five. Tony, another physician from New Haven, was introduced, as well as his companion, Nancy. Then followed Burt, a Yale drop-out who was once Jack's school mate and now a local race horse breeder. After the introductions, Okike and Mashangu were offered drinks. Mashangu asked for a dry Martini while Okike opted for a dry sherry.

That night, the guests were in for a later dinner. Jack and Stella took turns going downstairs to the kitchen to oversee the cooking. With drinks, rock and soul music, the conversation and laughter in the room became more boisterous as the evening wore on. 'Come off it you son of a . . . white man,' started Stella in a shrill voice. 'Go down and check the cooking.'

Jack shrugged his shoulders and stopped talking to Okike and said: 'You wanted to say son of a bitch didn't you? Okay, I am a son of a bitch, right? You Stella . . . are . . .'

Stella was quick to interpose before Jack could finish: '. . . a black bitch. That's what he was going to say. Shit man, why don't you people ever know how to say what's on your minds.'

Jack picked up his glass and slouched down to the kitchen. 'Whose turn is it to-night?' inquired Stella as her eyes darted across the room.

'Wait till I come up,' shouted Jack from downstairs. Everyone except Okike and Mashangu seemed to know what Stella was talking about. Mashangu and Okike exchanged glances and waited.

'Oh yes, I know whose turn it is . . . Sid. Last time it was Burt, remember?' continued Stella with visible relish. 'Remember the big birthmark on the right thigh Sid, come on, show it like it is. Come, let me give you a hand, You're not shy are you? Come,' continued Stella opening her arms broadly. 'Okike, look at the "elegant symmetry" of the Caucasian male . . . the nose . . . elegant isn't it?'

'Elegant symmetry, that's from Jefferson, right?' inquired Sid without much enthusiasm.

'Come on Sid, show it like it is. Give him some grass, music and a chick. I bet that will do the trick,' Burt said authoritatively.

'That's a non-starter,' Sid said emphatically.

'Oh, that's your aristocratic sense of decency.' Burt said despondently. As Jack walked in Stella said mockingly: 'Honey, no fun and games tonight, Sid won't budge, see.'

'Leave Sid alone . . . it's a free country. You watch a nude Caucasian body every night don't you?' asked Jack with some irritation in his tone.

As if to defuse the situation, Okike and Tony stood up to dance. They were joined by Nancy and Sid. Jack, Stella and Burt continued discussing the subject of nudity while Mashangu watched from his seat next to the fire. Reflectively he helped himself to more drink. Decadence . . . middle class decadence. Stella doesn't know it . . . she is bent on humiliating the white male . . . If only she were doing it consciously, in full possession of herself . . . impotent rage . . . the murderous impulse imprisoned in a suburban bedroom.

There was more talking, drinking and dancing in middle-class East-coast style until about two-thirty in the morning. In addition to the meal served at eleven, several rounds of drinks and 'pot' had been consumed. Mashangu had failed to get himself into the 'groove' and had alternated between an intense affection for Okike counterpointed by his loathing of Stella and her antics.

Little did he realise at the time that between these two black women was concentrated a conflict which was to rage in his mind for a long time to come. One part of the situation at the Skeltons dramatised for Mashangu the anguished soul of a dehumanised person of colour struggling with the beast inside — an encounter with the many shades of the impulse to violence. Okike represented to Mashangu, or so it seemed to him, that part of his nature which was fanatically attached to love, tenderness and the necessity for creating new life instead of destroying it.

The Violent Reverie

THE UNCONSCIOUS IN LITERATURE AND SOCIETY

If we substitute Erikson's nomination of the notions of *relativity* and the *unconscious* as two insights which provided 'disturbing extensions of human consciousness in our time' with tyranny and militant terrorism we introduce an immediate shift from the realm of ideas to that of raw everyday experience.[1] Militant terrorism and institutionalised tyranny constitute some of the raw experience of man in contemporary societies.

Terrorism in our time compels us to recognise unflinchingly the discrepancy between our knowledge and mastery of nature and our worn out half-truths about human nature. Clearly the ascendancy of violence in social action is related to a theme in contemporary life brought into focus by the Harvard psychiatrist Erik Erikson. In his pioneering studies of identity and human development, he has on a number of occasions drawn attention to what he terms pseudospeciation.[2] He has clarified for us some of the human uses of scapegoating — the creation of heroes and villains as orienting images in the development of open or closed group identities.

Such is the confusion of thought for action today that an American polemicist was obliged to say that 'it is, of course, scarcely possible to open the question of Israeli or Arab conduct today without exciting the most lively passion and risking the most serious charge.'[3] It should be added immediately that it is not only partisan *publics* which we may expect to find in most societies but career politicians who, like Tolstoy's generals, believe that they always know the meaning of social events as well as their prospective consequences.

The reactionary character of the resistence to intellectual scrutiny of societies and nations even in the free world is best exemplified by the international reaction to the rise of the third world. In the short history of the ascendancy of the third world into the international arena there have been ample opportunities for the study of how societies cling with a vigorous tenacity to outmoded images and identities. For the ascent of the third world has meant, amongst other things, that the identities of the world's non-Caucasian peoples should be transformed as part of the evolution from a predominantly subservient colonial status into new yet unstable identity con-stellations.

Beginning with Negritude in the 1930's and the notion of the *African personality* during the 1960's there emerged in the United States and later in South Africa the *black consciousness* movements. I want to suggest that these movements, dis-continuous as they appear and isolated both in temporal and geographic terms as they have been, are symptomatic of some profound need in the inner world of the black collective psyche to materialise a new identity to harness all the resources of its cultural and historical unconscious.

The psycho-historical propriety of these movements should by now have been fully established were it not for the com-peting and also deep-seated need mediating the older images which are required to survive in the service of pseudo-speciation. The historical impasse in the late twentieth century has now assumed the form of a confrontation between new images (emerging identities) created by strong psychological and spiritual needs against older images sustained by an equally strong psychological need for psychosocial domination (scapegoating) of subordinate by superordinate groups.

In the case of South Africa, the black consciousness move-ment as identity retrieval and creation emerged as the *antithesis* of the white dominant culture. Through an exclusive South Africanism, fragmentary as it appears at times, white South Africa has succeeded in mobilising a geo-political identity for itself since the Act of Union in 1910. With the exclusion of blacks from the broader South Africanism, the identity of blacks (Africans, Coloureds and Indians) remained hostage to prevailing white images of the people of colour which though revealing a local character are certainly no original creation of white South Africa.

With the unfolding of the historical process, including as well much that is irrational in it, the identity of blacks came to be invested, as is the rule in pseudospeciation, with the negative attributes of the white identity.

This is the point at which a statement regarding identity retrieval and creation should be made. Whether the reference is to *Negritude* or *black consciousness* as philosophy and social movement, the dynamic involved seems to be one in which a colossal attempt is made to help the victims of racialism to arrive at a more profound appreciation of their alienation, to unmask the limits of the false consciousness by unleashing for constructive purpose the welter of their 'unconscious resources.'

It is not true to the character of this impulse to be bound to vindictiveness of any kind since the momentum of such an impulse is inner-directed rather than other-directed. If vindictiveness is foreign to this impulse, anxiety is not. It is to be expected that as the people of colour agonise over their confrontation with their unconscious a communicative equivalence may arise to such an extent that more irrational ('primitive') responses may be expected from superordinates.[4] The profound challenge of black movements during this century on this continent and the *diaspora* amounts to the requirement for a frontal attack on the legacy of the unconscious so as to appreciate most fully the consequences of servitude and its companion — the false consciousness.

The unconscious as part of and mediator of the black experience (or any other for that matter) comes to constructive life in the literature, theatre and other arts of a people. This should remain true even at a most superficial level of analysis, for it is art at its best that explodes for our usually mundane consciousness those resonances which lie buried in man's innermost being. Art, like unconscious process, possesses the quality of shocking us out of our complacency by reflecting those contradictions and dimensions of human existence which prey on us while we sleep.

The themes which are hatched by these voices from limbo, like those of our dreams, are not partial to man's virtues. Naturally, much is brought to light which is diabolic in man. In the realms of art, the dream and reverie, nothing is beyond reach, impossible or inconceivable. Murders may be committed with complete abandon. Likewise, in our dreamlife, the most incompatible passions as well as the most contradictory notions are fused into terrifying unities. Most lay people and others not so lay would insist that our dreamlife makes little if any impact on what they believe to be the rational ordering of human communities. Yet the historically extreme situation such as we have at home in its compactness, demandingness and intolerableness forces the flood-gates of the unconscious into the open in one form of violence or another. Primitive fears of all kinds achieve mass circulation.

There is probably no comparable relationship which is as riddled with ambivalence, ambiguity and a potential for violence as that between a master and his slave. In this classical or prototypical instance of superordinancy and subordinancy is duplicated on an adult scale the whole psychology of subordination which since Freud's forays into childhood and the unconscious has become a little less baffling to us. In this study, only the bare outlines of this complex relationship will be touched on.

Psychoanalysis has taught us that the unconscious in its individual and collective variants is a legacy of both history and socialisation experience. The rearing of children (socialisation) over a long period of dependency is the longest in the animal kingdom and appears to get even longer with man's evolution in various subtle ways. The positive, that is, the health-giving elements, in this process of enabling the helpless and dependent child to prosper are well known to 'psychological man' and his 'therapeutic cultures.'[5] Negative unhealthy elements, on the other hand, to the extent that we know and understand them, are the stock-in-trade of the mental health professions in their encounters with failures of individual adaptation. The socialisation situation as we know it in most societies today is far from ideal.

The experience of *being* in infancy and early childhood with its characteristic dependency as well as the subsequent thriving of a sense of self is in itself of crucial significance yet, more often than not, it is this experience which becomes the first object of almost global amnesia. It is within such a context that we are able to see most clearly that the unconscious as legacy of socialisation depends for its development on this universal helplessness and dependency of the child and its adaptive need for amnesia. To the question why this cover-up is so crucial for this phase of human life several answers are possible. All the answers are, however, related to the fact that man begins his life in the face of overwhelming helplessness.[6] In the face of power-lessness and dependency, the emerging self is forced in the interests of its own survival and to cope with anxiety to initiate adaptive measures. During infancy and later, children insist on getting their own way — luxuriating in their feelings of omni-potence. But gradually this posture of the child is experienced as unequal to the demands of the adult social and physical universe including the child's *encounter and internalisation of authority relationships* with its parents. The impact of what is seen as an enabling intervention by parents slowly forces the child into new corrective, integrative and adaptive approaches primarily intended to contain rising levels of anxiety, conflict, aggression and grief at the loss of omnipotence. This primal loss of omnipotence is compensated for in an unsatisfactory but adaptive manner by the child's adoption of *ambivalence* towards the authority of parents and other adults. Adults and parents, for their own part, reward the child for this subversion of impulses natural to its condition on the basis of the pre-vailing arbitrary notions of 'good' and 'bad'.

It cannot be emphasised too strongly how in these two words is imbedded the seeds of what later becomes pathological in individual and group life.[7] Or as Norman O. Brown puts it:[8] 'Here is the fall: the distinction between "good" and "bad", between "mine" and "thine," between "me" and "thee" (or "it"), come all together — boundaries between persons; boundaries between properties; and the polarity of love and hate.' On the basis of its encounters with authority a child adopts this two-valued orientation, this crude distinction between good and bad as an axiomatic imperative for evaluating, regulating and ordering internal and interpersonal experience.

The saga of how a child emerges from its symbiotic dependency on its mother into a psycho-somatically differentiated self is a complex one.[9] It should suffice here merely to add the following considerations. One should readily admit that it is a poor preparation for life's 'little ironies' to begin with this two-valued orientation involving a categorical discrimination between good and bad for, among other things, it precludes the development of finer discriminations in evaluations of self, others and experience. In the twilight zone of infancy, therefore, may be laid some of the rugged foundations of later sterile and rigid sensibilities.

In struggling with its dependency, compensatory omnipotent strivings, the terrors of impending annihilation and aggressive impulses, the child is rewarded, as we have seen, for losing some of the battles with parental authority. The ensuing adaptation whether neurotic or 'healthy' assumes the character of ambivalence, this in the interests of circumvented high levels of anxiety and conflict so painstakingly documented by Melanie Klein and her followers.[10] Through psychological splitting which in my view is the symbolic equivalent of the physical and spatial differentiation of the body schema's inside-outside dimensions, parental figures are split and internalised as good and bad. The same father object becomes part good father and part bad father. This ambivalent adaptation also applies to the child's own evaluation and experience of self (self-representation) and there are good grounds for believing that it is this orientation which leaves the child with a polarised experience and representation of its body into a 'good' and pure upper body pole as against a 'bad' and impure lower pole.

There is sufficient room here only to suggest the complexity of the coming into being of the unconscious and its preference for encountering authority in a contradictory and ambivalent fashion. However, what seems necessary in the present context seems to be an indication that the unconscious assumes its hydra-like quality from the child's encounter with both its own utter dependency and the overwhelming authority of the agents of society.

To put the issue of the unconscious (whose origins I have attempted to outline) and art in historically extreme situations in its most basic form we need to examine the prototypical example of choice with respect to the issue of superordinancy and subordinancy. The relationship between a master and his slave is particularly informative because this relationship carries within it all the elements of a *symbiotic dehumanisation* (Camus' community of victims) as well as the seeds of a non-metaphysical rebellion. We never stop wondering why it is that the slave indulges himself to the extent of making the task of dehumanisation easier for his master by consistently, indeed one is tempted to say religiously, colluding with the master in the slave's own harrassment.

It may be said that this primarily unconscious collusion is something which goes against or must be seen against the slave's own conscious attitude since, it may be suggested, the slave does protest too much. But the reactionary character of such protest becomes apparent since its form is always benign enough as to ensure that the self-sustaining symbiotic relationship is left intact.

The central dilemma in the psychology of subordination both in its infantile (natural) and adult forms is the fear of losing ambivalence (subjective violence) for violence as social act — a transformation considered by the subject as possible both within the realm of unconscious fantasy and in reality. In both situations, those of the child encountering parental authority and that of the slave face to face with the authority of his master, ambivalence is predicated and sustained by violence against the self to placate once and for all the alternative in favour of objective violence against the representatives of authority. The unconscious, dialectical approach to reality is at its most powerful in this instance since violent impulse is bound up with the tenderest concern and affection for the object of hate. The ambivalent character of adaptation under conditions of subordination is maximised by its psychic precariousness — the anxiety about talion (retaliation) and the lingering possibility that subjective violence may without sufficient warning be transformed into violence as social act.

A formulation such as the one presented above has sound clinical backing in treatment situations and as psychotherapists we have become familiar with the various neurotic and sometimes psychotic ways in which individuals bring to a catastrophic denouement this universal childhood problem of ambivalence.

What has been said thus far has implied without explicitness that between ambivalence and objective violence (violence as social act) there often emerges under conditions of long subordination of one group by another a committed literature. At the level of the social *praxis* a literature of stature must emerge to mediate the dissonances between violence against the self and violence as social act.

Western literary critics have often drawn and continue to draw distinctions between African literature and that of the West. Implied and explicitly stated at times is the idea that, amongst other things, the limitations in African literature are those of range of themes and innovations in technique of presentation. Writing about 'African novels,' Per Wästberg has this to say:[11]

> 'In most of them, the narrative is restrained and non-experimental, and character takes second place to situation and plot. An individual's emotional conflicts are seldom a central element. Nowhere in African literature, for example, do we find a gripping description of love or a great tragedy.'

Nadine Gordimer in *The Black Interpreters* echoes the words of Per Wästberg as follows:[12]

> 'The thematic preoccupation of many white writers in the world today is no, no, no; without a "yes," without positive affirmation of any kind to follow. Country boy coming to town says "no" to his exploitation there, "no" to his secondclass status in the competitive white world; but he does not turn his back on that world; opt out, even when he realises that the world he left behind in his tribal village has a value he must not lose or fail to assert, either. The African hero . . . despite his disaffection and bitterness, is a man who says yes and yes and yes . . . The angry young man of European novels of the fifties and early sixties does not exist in African literature. Neither does that other darling of English and American contemporary fiction, the

man or woman, often an academic, in whom the fruits of mass culture and/or intellectual privilege have produced a sour fermentation of disillusion with the material satisfactions offered by an affluent, industrial society. The Been-To suffers, but he is not sick at heart. He believes that things have gone wrong; not that they are inherently wrong, built on a foundation of moral decay. Another European theme that has no place in African literature is that of the problem of communication itself . . . In Africa, it seems, the lines are still clear.'

This engthy comparative statement, condescending as it is in part, is followed by the pronouncement: 'Black writers choose their plots, characters and literary styles; their themes choose them.'

I must admit that at first sight the last part of this statement appeared compellingly convincing. Here I thought, is a profound insight. But a little recollection of the history of man in revolt such as Camus has provided us with coupled with what we have recently learnt and are learning about the psychology of the colonised, led to further reflection on the question. I do not want to appear to be creating a storm in a tea cup but the issues involved here are of such importance that even a passing reference should turn out to be rewarding.

There is a sense in which no writer chooses his themes or the images which crowd his consciousness prior, during and after the creation of a work of art. Since the creative impulse tends to straddle itself across several layers of the individual's consciousness, the act of *choosing* is part of a more cognitive set of conditions and at the tail-end of the process and probably not part of the incubative stage. Another way of conceptualising the events involved here is to say that it seems more likely that themes, images and reveries are not arbitrary since in the ultimate analysis the writer must draw from the collective cultural consciousness (including that which is unconscious) of his people and should he be a prominent writer, he can add new nuances and dimensions to such a consciousness.

The intellectual history of the west suggests that human development is guided by a simple and pragmatic principle. Although this principle is simple in its immediate clarity its sources in the human psyche are organised around the principle of 'hierarchy of prepotency' of human needs and motives.[13] The idea that human consciousness as it expresses itself cognitively, spiritually, in social action and historically thrives on the destruction of any opposition to its dominant position should certainly not be taken for a novel idea. Hegel seems to have been the first man, as far as I know, to have recognised and formulated this incorporative and, by the same token, destructive quality of human consciousness. Depending on the context, this encounter with oppositional reality is effected on a symbolic and/or social level.

The important insight which should emerge from an acceptance of this characterisation of human consciousness is that consciousness begins its destruction of opposition with the most immediate object and widens the circles to the ultimate bounds, which in the case of Western man is Creation itself. Is it surprising that whilst Western man has been struggling to kill God, people of colour have been concentrating their attention on the church instead? It may be instructive at this point to make an observation with a substantiating quote.

From my own experience, I endorse the view of Sartre who, writing about anti-Semitism and the Jew, suggests that owing to his special history and situation the Jew has not yet been allowed to be integrated into world society. He is not, to put it plainly, simply a man. That is to say that he is not defined in terms other than his jewishness. In Sartre's own words:[14]

> The disquietude of the Jew is not metaphysical; it is social. The ordinary object of his concern is not yet the place of man in the universe, but his place in society. He cannot perceive the loneliness of each man in the midst of a silent universe, because he has not yet emerged from society into the world. It is among men that he feels himself lonely; the racial problem limits his horizon. Nor is his uneasiness of the kind that seeks perpetuation; he takes no pleasure in it — he seeks reassurance . . .
>
> It is society, not the decree of God, that has made him a Jew and brought the Jewish problem into being. As he is forced to make his choices within the perspective set by his problem, it is in and through the social that he chooses even his own existence. His constructive effort to integrate himself in the national community is social; social is the effort he makes to think of

himself, that is, to situate himself, among other men; his joys and sorrows are social; but all this is because the curse that rests upon him is social. If in consequence he is reproached for his metaphysical inauthenticity, if attention is called to the fact that his constant uneasiness is accompanied by a radical positivism, let us not forget that these reproaches return upon those who make them: the Jew is social because the anti-Semite has made him so.

I think that what Sartre says about the situation of the Jew applies with equal force to the situation of the man of colour. African literature may at this point in history be thriving on a 'radical positivism' by being a literature of the socially pragmatic. Is there any reason for the surprise implicit in Nadine Gordimer's statement?

It is this 'radical positivism' which gives rise to a committed literature. To ask and expect blacks to abandon this radical positivism for a sterile and unpromising metaphysics of a world they have not yet entered is like asking a semi-starved man to exchange his loaf of bread for a ticket to a concert of chamber music. By adopting a radical positivism — letting their creativity emerge from the resonances and dissonances of the socio-political fabric of which they are a part, black writers remain rooted and true to the themes struggling for expression, resolution and clarification in the consciousness of their people.

Unless we understand this radical positivism of the oppressed and the psychological conditions which nourish it we are unlikely to appreciate fully creations such as the fragments at the beginning of this book or the following passage written years ago by a famous black writer:[15]

> We broke down the doors. The master's room was wide open. The master's room was brilliantly lighted, and the master was there, quite calm . . . and we stopped . . . He was the master . . . I entered. 'It is you,' he said to me, quite calmly . . . It was I. It was indeed I, I told him, the good slave, the faithful slave, the slavish slave, and suddenly his eyes were two frightened cockroaches on a rainy day . . . I struck, the blood flowed: That is the only baptism I remember today.

What are we to make of a murder represented creatively with almost clinical precision? Anger, resentment, ambivalent feelings and the impulse to violence must present themselves under diverse situations in the lives of members of subordinate groups. In between these primarily unconscious themes which occasionally seek objective expression in social action such as a politically motivated assassination or a terrorist blood-bath such as we have become accustomed to in the late twentieth century is to be found the 'mask' or what I prefer to call the *false consciousness*.

This false consciousness which consists of the proverbial smile of the colonised, the expressionless face in the wake of intense provocation and the unconscious collusion with superordinates in the former's dehumanisation is the expression in social action of a corresponding ambivalence in the subjective lives of subordinates. It appears as if there are two main avenues open to subordinates once the conditions are ripe for unmasking this false consciousness.

For the rank and file, the path from subjective violence against the self to violence against others, in particular superordinates and their *symbolic representations,* may on occasion be a very short one. Psychologically and particularly from the psychoanalytic intuition this *tour de force* occasions little surprise. What is regarded as 'acting out' in psychoanalytic psychotherapy is extremely informative with regard to the issue under immediate consideration. The patient who 'acts out' is resistant to the therapist's efforts at helping him to transform non-premeditated action of unconscious origin into language form such as to correspond to conscious thoughts and feelings the patient should entertain.[16]

This resistance to the therapist's intervention is occasioned by the unconscious' preference for action on a reckless and sometimes large scale. It is as if the individual who is acting out were saying that action should come before understanding and explanation that is, before language. Individuals participating in a riot appear to be acting similarly since even here language, to the extent that it mediates understanding, explanation and conventional modes of dealing with social reality, is suspended. In psychoanalytic terms it could be said that the impulse to violence as *primary process* (unconscious) short-circuits language and cognitive elements, the so-called *secondary process,* in its instant transformation into action during the act of violent rebellion. During this transformation, not only are secondary processes non-functional but in addition, the twin emotion in the spectrum of ambivalence is also undermined to such an extent that the violent act is the more potent in proportion to the experienced elimination of ambivalence.

In rebellion, the act becomes charismatic in that it achieves for the subject instantly the important aims of *focusing* and *ritualisation* so significant for the elimination of ambivalence.[17]

The violent rebellious act appears to be more importantly a product of a chronic, silent and secret anguish. Once the act is committed the subject experiences a perverse kind of purgation since both the impulse and its consequent act are universalised. It is this insight which led Camus to say in writing about a 'community of victims' that 'it is for the sake of everyone in the world that the slave asserts himself when he comes to the conclusion that a command has infringed on something in him which does not belong to him alone, but which is common ground where all men — even the man who insults and oppresses him — have a natural community.[18] Is it not true that the natural community as opposed to the 'community of victims' is the universal community of man?

One could say that the black writer as a radical positivist is located midway between historical and metaphysical rebellion. He differs from his brethen to the extent that in his case the silent and secret anguish forms itself finally into images and not as is the case with the slave into instant action during a propitious moment. The image does not present itself in its fullness without a period of gestation. The artist like his brethren must come to terms with ambivalence, self-intoxicating resentment and violence against the self. In his case, however, it can be noticed that the short-circuit we referred to above fails to occur. The unconscious is directed towards a more creative course and thereby allows language to mediate between itself and possible acting out in the social sphere.

For the artist, therefore, the creative act itself assumes the same importance which the violent and/or rebellious act assumes for the common rebel. The image(s) forces itself from formlessness into clarity and through the creative act the artist also transforms subjective experience into the realm of the universal — the natural community. The artist is enchanted by the charisma of an image.

An implicit contradiction may have suggested itself to the astute reader by this time. It will shortly be evident that such a contradiction is more apparent than real and does not require a radical dialectic for its clarification.

Can it be said of the artist that he is a radical positivist if it can also be demonstrated that he is more enchanted by images rather than action? His first solution for the problem of sub-ordination and its consequent violent and rebellious impulse is symbolic rather than actual. He responds at a more primitive level by placing his whole weight behind ritualisation on a symbolic level in the place of a real murder as a social act. To come back to the black writer of repute whom we quoted earlier we immediately recognise as we look more closely the writer's reverence in the face of the symbolic. Indeed, I think we should say there is a ritualistic precision in the manner in which the slave slaughters his previous master. In this short passage is concentrated all the major elements of an act as ritual. Ritual has several important uses in the affairs of man and one of these uses is that of clarification — of subverting with due courtesy such imponderables as death. It is notable that the murder portrayed in the passage is not rash but executed with a cold calculation that is undergirded with veneration. The outcome consists of both clarity and a new level of confidence or, shall we say, authenticity? The 'I' after the ritual is no longer a 'grammatical fiction.'

The artists' elimination of the 'I' as grammatical fiction by subduing the impulse to violence into a shocking but realistic image has consequences for social action or representations of the self in public which restore to the artist his identity as a radical positivist.

What, we are entitled to ask, is the pragmatic value of this ritual murder which attaches itself to such disturbing images? To begin with, this ritualisation which takes the artist to the outer limits of the violent and rebellious reverie in undermining ambivalence, and by the same token violence to the self, erodes the false consciousness at its core. Even though this intuition remains true in fundamental respects it may be argued by those who attach serious significance to the fascinating split between the objective and the subjective that such a psycho-spiritual culmination amounts to nothing since objectively the artist remains, in the case of blacks at least, a member of a subordinate group and unfree.

Though appealing such a view suffers from the shortcomings of a radical reductionism since we now know that subordination over time involves not only structural instrumentalities of dominance but also *psycho-social instrumentalities,* the latter being in the final analysis the most dehumanising.

The radical positivism of the literature of the oppressed arises from the fact that ideally it achieves for the artist and his readership a long-term unmasking of the false consciousness. It invalidates the competing cleavages in the self of the man of colour enabling him to break the symbiotic chain between him and his superordinates, thus clearing the way for a natural community as opposed to the community of victims. The master is assassinated in the realm of reverie and the seductive image to enable the subordinate to live realistically and authentically with superordinates in the social sphere.

I have made the claim that the violent reverie may be put to constructive social use by the people of colour. In making this point I choose for special emphasis two aspects. The first of these is that the violent reverie in its painful gestation over time and its ultimate instantaneous blossoming into metaphysical murder as ritualisation creates unity in the psychic economy of subordinate individuals by dispelling an immobilising ambivalence. It makes it possible for the slave to live with himself but more importantly with his master. Since with the transformation the slave says: 'It is I . . . It is indeed I,' his master is bound to respond to the new reality in whatever way is most propitious at the time.

Secondly, the constructive use of the violent reverie prepares the way for the superordinate victim to recognise and appreciate the subordinate victim at a more profound level than was possible before. Sentimental rationalisations for the familiar ordering of the slave-master symbiosis are placed under severe strain by the new identity of the slave as rebel.

Today, perhaps more than ever before, it has become imperative to bridge the experiential gap between Negrophobes and blacks both here and in the *diaspora*. Such an achievement could sustain painfully-won victories in the spheres of tolerance, mutual respect and understanding as well as ensure that these victories are not spurious but long-lasting. From the violent reverie must be allowed to emerge a literature virile enough to touch us (despite some initial shock, disbelief or anxiety) where it matters most — the innermost core which informs our relations in public. We should never assume without serious reflection that the cold fire or ritual murder which gather around the violent reverie are without emotional sting or impact. Nor is it necessary to wait for the arsonist's flame before we take the constructive elements of the violent reverie into account.

The black reader who is confronted with Mashangu's violent reveries or those of Césaire quoted above will be struck by their enticing but terrifying familiarity. On the other hand, we can expect non-blacks to be shocked by what may at first sight appear to be excesses of an inflamed imagination. When all is said and done we ignore, suppress and abort the violent reverie and the subsequent image at our own peril. The African writer as radical positivist can say prophetically: 'weep not for me but for yourself and your children', and, we should add emphatically, for our children.

NOTES:
1. Erik Erikson in his *Dimensions of a New Identity* (New York, 1974) writes: 'In fact, I would nominate the idea of relativity in the physical world and the concept of the unconscious in man's inner world (and I include in this Marx's discovery of a class unconscious) as two such disturbing extensions of human consciousness in our time. And I would postulate that any new identity must develop the *courage of its relativities and the freedom of its unconscious resources;* which includes facing the anxiety aroused by both.' p. 103.
2. For a wide-ranging discussion of pseudospeciation in the context of competing group identities see Erikson: *Dimensions of a New Identity,* ibid. and with H. Newton: *In Search of Common Ground* (New York,

1973). Erikson's notion of pseudospeciation (scapegoating) is clearly illustrated in the following brief extracts from his *Dimensions of a New Identity* in which he writes: 'But, alas, the new identity (that of American pioneers), to define itself, also needs some people *below*, who must be kept in their place, confined, or even put away. For in order to live up to a new self, a man always needs an otherness to represent at the bottom of the social scale that *negative identity* which each person and each group carries within it as a sum of all that it must not be.' p. 36. Later, he adds: 'But, alas, as we also emphasised, man always needs somebody who is below him, who will be kept in place, and on whom can be projected all that is felt to be weak, low, and dangerous in oneself. If Americans had not had the Indians and the blacks — who far from having conquered their land could not defend it, or who, far from having wanted to come here had been forced to — the new Americans would have had to invent somebody else in their place.' p. 78. For other stimulating discussions of this theme see Kovel's *White Racism: A Psychohistory* (New York: 1970) and Neumann's: *Depth Psychology and New Ethic* (New York, 1973). Neumann for example has this to say about pseudospeciation: 'In the economy of the psyche, the outcast role of the alien is immensely important as an object for the projection of the shadow — that part of our personality which is 'alien' to the ego, our own unconscious counter-position, which is subversive of our conscious attitude and security — can be exteriorised and subsequently destroyed.' p. 52.

3. This observation is attributed to the American polemicist Berrigan in the April 1974 issue of *Ramparts,* p. 11.

4. During periods of crisis when the superordinate-subordinate symbiosis is threatened by some action on the part of the subordinate a state of subjective equivalence is usually manifest in what is often referred to as 'over-reaction' on the part of those in authority. This may account for the fact that the so-called 'protest literature' is often found to be so disturbing by those in power. Since this over-reaction is often unequal to the objective situation, it seems reasonable to assume that it has its origins in the unconscious realm of primitive fantasies.

5. See Philip Rieff's: *The Triumph of the Therapeutic: Uses of Faith After Freud* (New York, 1966).

6. Although many outstanding psychoanalytic observers such as Winnicott have discussed the dependency of the infant no one to my knowledge has been as convinced about the helplessness of the infant during the first year of life as Neumann who in his *The Child: Structure and Dynamics of the Nascent Personality* (New York, 1973) writes of the child as living through a 'social uterine' or post-natal 'embryonic' period.

7. Discriminations between 'good' and 'bad' are part of the complex symbolic matrix which is at the core of the process of scapegoating.

8. Brown, N. *Love's Body* (New York, 1966) p. 143. In his characteristically cryptic style in *Love's Body* he explains scapegoating in the following terms: 'there is only one psyche, in relation to which all conflict is endopsychic, all war intestine. The external enemy is (part of) ourselves, projected; our own badness, banished. The only defense against an internal danger is to make it an external danger: then we can fight it; and are ready to fight it, since we have succeeded in deceiving

ourselves into thinking it is no longer us.' p. 162.

9. The complexity of the early experiences of the child is due in part to the fact that in infancy we are privileged to witness the interface between the symbolic and the bodily as these are represented in the needs of the child and the caretaking activities of a mother.

10. See for example Klein, M. *Envy and Gratitude and Other Works 1946-1963* (London, 1975) in particular: 'Notes on some schizoid Mechanisms' pp. 1-24.

11. See Wästberg, P. 'Themes in African Literature Today' (Spring, 1974) p. 139.

12. See Gordimer, N. *The Black Interpreters* (Johannesburg 1973), pp. 9 and 11.

13. In motivation theory as advocated by the late American psychologist Maslow, the satisfaction of basic needs such as physiological needs predictably leads to the ascendancy of high-order needs such as those for self-esteem and self-actualisation. Human Consciousness, bound as it is to human needs and by the same token motivation, appears to be guided by a similar principle — one of immediacy.

14. See Sartre, J. P. *Anti-Semite and Jew* (New York: 1948) pp. 134-135.

15. This passage is cited by Fanon, F. in his *Black Skin White Masks* (New York: 1967) p. 198.

16. 'Acting out' in the context of psychoanalytic therapy refers to the tendency of patients in some situations to act on the basis of the first and most immediate impulse. Jerome Singer in his discussion of 'The Vicissitudes of Imagery in Research and Clinical Use' (Spring: 1971) has this to say about acting out: 'He (the patient) learns soon that, when he experiences a sudden irrational fear or burst of rage, the appropriate thing to do is to quietly replay in his mind's eye his own sequence of thought. Usually this will reveal the specific memory or transference distortion that triggered the emotion, and the use of the replay method averts action on the basis of the first impulse, which could lead to fatal consequences.' p. 167.

17. See Erikson, E. *Ghandhi's Truth* (New York: 1969) for a discussion of the significance of ritualisation.

18. Camus, A. *The Rebel* (New York: 1956) p. 16.

REFERENCES

BROWN, N. 1966 *Love's Body,* New York: Vintage Books.

CAMUS, A. *The Rebel,* New York: Vintage Books.

ERIKSON, E. 1969 *Gandhi's Truth: On the Origins of Militant Nonviolence.* New York: Norton, Inc., 1974 *Dimensions of a New Identity,* New York: Norton, Inc.

ERIKSON, E. & H. NEWTON, 1973 *In Search of Common Ground,* New York: Norton, Inc.

FANON, F. 1967 *Black Skin White Masks,* New York: Grove Press.

GORDIMER, N. 1973 *The Black Interpreters,* Johannesburg: Sprocas-Ravan.

KLEIN, M. 1975 *Envy and Gratitude and Other Works 1946-1963,* London: Hogarth Press.

KOVEL, J. 1970 *White racism: A Psychohistory,* New York: Vintage Books.

NEUMANN, E. 1973 *The child: structure and Dynamics of the Nascent Personality*. Trns. R. Mannheim. New York: G. Putnam's Sons. 1973 *Depth Psychology and a New Ethic*. New York: Harper Torchbooks.

RIEFF, P. 1966 *The triumph of the Therapeutic: Uses of Faith After Freud*, New York: Harper Torchbooks.

SARTRE, J. 1948 *Anti-Semite and Jew*, New York: Schocken Books.

SINGER, J. 'The Vicissitudes of Imagery in Research and Clinical Use.' *Contemporary Psychoanalysis*, 7, 2, 163-180.

WÄSTERBERG, P. 1974 'Themes in African Literature Today.' *Daedalus*. Spring, 135-150.

PART II

Two Essays

The Baptism of Fire

SOUTH AFRICA'S BLACK MAJORITY AFTER THE
PORTUGUESE COUP

The remnants of the Portuguese colonial empire crumbled in 1974. This important event in the history of imperialism and colonial racism in Southern Africa must still be studied as contemporary history. The human drama in which the Portuguese coup was the historical denouement is currently accessible to us only in vague outline. Perhaps nothing else in recent history dramatises so well the elements of contingency and ambiguity in the historical process — the emergence on the historical scene of the unexpected.

With regard to the probable impact of the Portuguese coup and the subsequent decolonisation process on Southern Africa and its peoples, it seems prudent to assert with Merleau-Ponty that nobody has any science of the future.[1] The future, unlike the past, is always probable — but not in the reassuring statistical sense of that word. Given the problem suggested by Merleau-Ponty's statement, the social sciences use what is current and known (however dimly) to understand and delineate emerging and probable historical developments. This social science of the probable means walking on quicksand and losing ground all the time. Nonetheless, in full conviction and conscious awareness, it remains possible to project into the dimness of the future some plausible directions which phenomena such as political loyalties and self-identities may assume in the arena of group and/or race conflict.

These considerations constitute a baseline for the

examination of the following topics:

> some methodological issues in the study of subordinancy and superordinancy:
>
> multiple siege cultures — the South African case;
>
> prophets, academics, and the 'dustbin' revolt;
>
> the future of the race supremacist ethos;
>
> the 'eclipse of reason.'

ISSUES IN THE STUDY OF SUBORDINANCY AND SUPERORDINANCY

Contemporary societies under stress often turn to social science scholarship for direction and guidance. Although this distress signal is often muted, its existence in a society is easily detected in the restlessness of social scientists. Southern Africa after the Portuguese coup is not exceptional in this regard. More than any other professional group, sociologists in Southern Africa show notable restlessness. A note of urgency creeps into the themes they examine. In addition to the exploration of methodological problems in the study of attitudes,[2] themes range from a re-examination of sociological perspectives for the study of race,[3] consideration of research opportunities, and problems for social science research in divided societies.[4]

Several things must be said about this research on subordinancy and superordinancy. First, social science research about race relations requires the active participation of researchers who are themselves members of subordinate groups.[5] Second, because of the unsophisticated level of theory in the study of attitudes and the methodological problems encountered in its use, it becomes difficult to give a full-dress assessment of the several important South African studies of attitudes.[6]

Nonetheless, there are two basic orientations which may be adopted in the study of situations of asymmetrical power relationships which lead to a superordinate-subordinate social structure. One orientation relates to objective social conditions: group cleavages, problems, and conflict over power and resource allocation in the economic, political, and military spheres. The other orientation points toward more elusive sub-

jective conditions — experiences, cognitions, value orientations, perceptions of self and others — which exist as
equivalents of the objective structural arrangements within a
society. Sometimes a half-hearted attempt is made to capture
reality at both levels, but not often enough and not satis-
factorily either.[7]

In South African society with its clearly-demarcated
domains of permissible experience, whites (members of superordinate groups) studying blacks (subordinates) find themselves face to face with an experiential hiatus of such
magnitude as to denude their personal experience as a resource
for both hypothesis formation and the meaningful interpretation of data. The implication of this point was summed up
cogently by another psychologist in a different, but related
context:

> The task of the psychologist is to understand people by making
> explicit what people can communicate to him concerning their
> experience and behaviour. In order to make meaningful
> explications he will continually draw on his own experience
> which will have been built up out of his own dialogue with the
> world and fellow man.[8]

In studies of attitudes and perceptions of self and others (the
main concern here), as well as potential behaviour growing
from these attitudes and perceptions, the researcher must (in
the face of these unfavourable conditions) paradoxically
undertake more than is usually required. In the study of the
social psychology of superordinancy and subordinancy, facing
several intermediate (and often unknown) variables between
the existence of an attitude and its expression in language and
behaviour, the researcher must conceive of his scholarly
responsibility to make explicit the unconscious, or pro-
conscious.

Thus, a plea for an inter-disciplinary approach to the
problems of race is as refreshing as it is challenging.[9] For it
must be remembered that white researchers may find in their
studies of black reactions and adaptions to racial
subordination a *false consciousness*.[10] It seems unlikely that
social science in South Africa will unmask it. The task might be
easier, if a literature of the oppressed were actively encouraged

or, at least, allowed to survive.[11] Such literature could help social science, because the creative impulse derives its momentum from various levels and dimensions of human consciousness, including the innermost core — the realm of the collective unconscious. In any case, social science would contribute much, if it did no more than introduce a rational ethos into the discourse about social reality in historically-extreme situations like South Africa.

MULTIPLE SIEGE CULTURES:
THE SOUTH AFRICAN CASE

Afrikaner intellectuals may study South African history and Afrikaner history for purely patriotic reasons, but the contemporary generation of black intellectuals studies the same history for a different purpose: to understand better how the Afrikaner struggle for freedom, often noble in its earliest manifestations, could have turned so negative by the 1970s.[12] One black observer said recently that the Afrikaner dilemma now consists of Afrikaner nationalism's failure to come to terms with the implied consequences of its own struggles and spiritual history.[13]

The development of Afrikaner *volksnasionalisme* has been compared usefully to 'white cultures under siege' in the southern U.S. and in present-day Rhodesia:

> The threatened group envisions a society based on its values and belief system. Dependent upon the society's structural arrangements and the group's own power compared to that of the threatening group (or groups), the siege culture will pursue diverse strategies (dependent upon its own dominant or subordinate position in society) aimed at the preservation or implementation of its culture and belief system. The siege culture evolves a defensive ideology or belief system that (a) articulates contrasting conceptions that distinguish between 'we' (the siege culture) and 'they' (the threatening group or groups), (b) serves as the basis for establishing group solidarity in the face of the perceived threat, and (c) provides a rationale or justification for its actions and mobilisation efforts. The greater the perceived threat, the greater the possibility that the belief system (reflected thereafter in the behaviour of the group) of the siege culture will become more rigid, dogmatic, and closed.[14]

The threats to the Afrikaner culture and belief system arose from changing circumstances in the history of South Africa. The most important perceived threats were the intrusive policies imposed by the British imperial administration after annexation of the Cape in 1806 and the presence of African traditional societies which, apart from being racially and culturally different, challenged Boer expansionism with force. Afrikaner history admits of a close (and alarming) resemblance to classical Aristotelian tragedy. Such tragedy encompasses a charismatic nobility and eminent courage, accompanied by a parasitic *harmatia* (weakness of the great). Is it putting it too strongly to say that Afrikanerdom, at the height of its power, is embroiled in a struggle to resolve this tragic contest between strength and weakness?[15]

If a recent paper by a Stellenbosch philosopher, J. Degenaar, can be a guide, enlightened Afrikaners will find little serious fault with the idea of an Afrikaner siege culture. Degenaar suggests that fear of cultural extinction led to the development of Afrikaner *volksnasionalisme,* a 'value-oriented movement' which later became a 'closed system' of ideas and beliefs. The myth of a God-given identity was also significant and accounts in part for the continued exclusivity of Afrikaner values:

> Although the myth of the chosen people is not generally applied to the Afrikaner today, the policy of separate development is very much rooted in the idea of the identity of the Afrikaner that should be protected . . . Afrikaner nationalism is still based on this *volksnasionalisme,* in that it cannot accommodate English-speaking whites, Afrikaans-speaking Coloureds, the Indians, and the urban and urbanised Africans. *Volksnasionalisme,* which can work in a homogeneous society, is clearly in a paradigmatic crisis when confronted with a heterogeneous society of multi-ethnic and multi-racial complexity. This paradigmatic crisis is indeed one of the basic problems facing the Afrikaner in South Africa today.[16]

One interesting thought should be noted here. It is meaningless to talk of a country facing a crisis, if that crisis is in fact occurring in one segment of the society. For the Afrikaner, the *volk* ideology has outlived its usefulness as an emancipatory concept by turning into a tool for Afrikaner domination of others. In so doing, it has become an 'oppressive concept . . . also for the Afrikaners.'[17]

A natural progression in the evolution of siege cultures seems evident. There are honourable beginnings in the desire of a group for freedom and survival as a cultural entity. Then, the group experiences strong psychological, social, and economic pressures to single itself out for a special dispensation in which all the negative attributes in its own identity are projected onto any other groups in the society which are subordinate.[18] But in a heterogeneous society, when any one group develops a strong, exclusive, and oppressive group identity, other groups will also try to do so. As a result, tensions develop in the superordinancy-subordinancy pattern. The dominant group becomes even more oppressive in its effort to squelch the rise of competitive group identities.

South Africa contains several siege cultures. The Afrikaner culture evolved in this general pattern until it reached its current position of dominance. On the other hand, Blacks have only recently started to articulate an acute perception of threats to their own cultural and group survival. Since the beginning of the 1970s, they have begun also to mobilise themselves into a 'value-oriented movement', with similar attributes of exclusiveness, dogmatism, and a tendency toward a closed system.

The development of an urban black siege culture represents a crisis for Afrikaner *volksnasionalisme,* because this competing group identity and nationalism — despite its emulation of the Afrikaner's historical example — increases Afrikaner perception of threat to their own survival as a *volk.* The present consideration of some kind of Afrikaner incorporation of English-speaking whites, Coloureds, and even Indians, in an effort to forestall the black challenge, paradoxically in itself threatens the Afrikaner *volk.* A heroic reappraisal of *volksnasionalisme* is required to resolve this dilemma.

The ascendancy of an urban black siege culture depends not only on the dominant white siege culture. The withdrawal of the Portuguese from Mozambique and Angola generated powerful symbols of African nationalist achievement. The power and proximity of these symbols have important psychological implications. African 'front-line' leadership, regardless of the merits of its ideological posture, has emerged as aggressive and more charismatic than the leadership perceived earlier in the immediately-neighbouring black states. The standards against which local black leadership is assessed have thus been raised, with the short-term result that gaps will develop between some present black readers and their followers.

Another factor of importance is the issue of formal identity vis-a-vis informal identity now posed squarely by homeland independence and citizenship. Black formal identity is defined by the evolving priorities of Afrikaner Nationalist political solutions to South African ethnic problems. Black informal identity is another matter altogether, particularly in the cities:

> Has 'de-ethnisation' in Soweto then proceeded beyond the point of no return? The government emphasises 'homeland links' and tries to propagate 'national' identifications. The evidence suggests that it is too late for this kind of political ethnicity; its place is likely to be taken more and more by black ethnicity.[19]

It is this 'black ethnicity' which, as an informal rallying point, will create about it the elements necessary for the consolidation of an urban black siege culture. This new siege culture will face two strong pressures: continued, and perhaps growing oppression from the Afrikaner siege culture; and a developing cleavage between urban blacks and rural blacks, which will pose difficulties for the consolidation of a still-larger black siege culture.[20]

PROPHETS, ACADEMICS, AND THE 'DUSTBIN' REVOLT

The Oxford don, A. H. Halsey, once introduced an article on research into British race relations this way:

> The most obvious question to ask about the black British is: will they revolt? All previous questions seem to lead to this one. And however circumlocutory the phrasing, this must surely be posed . . . a convincing answer would be fabulously cheap . . . to both social theorists of order and conflict and those directly engaged in race relations practice.[21]

This question, posed so bluntly for Britain in 1970, usually appears in the South African context in muted and 'circumlocutory . . . phrasing.' Nonetheless, it lurks behind most private and public thinking and action about race in South Africa. White researchers have focused on it. Lever dismisses the possibility of black revolt with a listing of black deficiencies which includes 'a lack of motivation to actively oppose the system.'[22] Schlemmer gives the question more intelligent and systematic attention. Although he suggests some increase in black resentment and hostility toward whites since the 1957 Biesheuvel study, he legitimately notes that his own data does not entitle him to give a definitive answer.[23]

Black observers tend to be unequivocal in their analysis, because of their personal immersion in subordinate social circumstances. They believe a violent racial confrontation is inevitable, unless major social-political change takes place in South Africa.[24]

The question of black revolt must take on a new form and its answering greater urgency after the 1976 urban black revolt. Instead of 'will they revolt?', the question now must be, 'what strategies for change are likely to emerge on the South African scene after the 1976 'dustbin' revolt?'

To what extent will the present urban revolt have consequences in the mobilisation of black resources? In the longer-term (although perhaps not in the short-term), the dominant group must consider the self-destructive implications of reliance on oppression to ensure its own dominance. Oppressed groups learn to live with violence. It then changes from a deterrent to an incentive, especially for the young and rebellious. There is a grim omen in the 'dustbin' revolt: unarmed, even apolitical young men and women found a grim satisfaction in this baptism of fire. They are unlikely to forget their initiation into revolt through violent means.

The most important lesson of what started in Soweto on 16 June 1976 can best be appreciated as a black challenge to psychological domination by Afrikaner *volksnasionalisme*.[25] Blacks in South Africa recognise the short-term difficulties of changing the pattern of structural dominance, although the inherent power of sheer numbers will prove increasingly effective. Nonetheless, it is the psychological domination of blacks by whites that will diminish first, leaving, after a while, the underlying issue of structural dominance more apparent.

The 1976 disturbances will also have 'demonstration effects.' Blacks and Coloureds now have a larger awareness of their capability for mobilisation and challenge of the regime. With psychological domination undermined, it will become easier to mobilise group resources in pressure-strikes, boycotts, violence, or even warfare — or competition — by the manipulation of labour and skills required by the dominant group.[26] In this light, the 1973 Durban strikes involved an early attempt to use competitive resources to secure change, while the 1976 revolt mobilised both pressure and competitive resources.

There is an important lesson in the pattern of resource mobilisation during the 1976 revolt about the relative influence of formal and informal leadership in black urban communities. The formal leadership is identified with government-created institutions and policies, and it therefore suffers from a lack of legitimacy and credibility among urban blacks. On the other hand, the informal leadership grows out of the 1970s black renaissance and is closely-identified with the growing black siege culture. These leaders are effective, but they lack any status or influence in dealing with the government and easily become scapegoats for governmental reprisals after crises occur. The danger of effective leadership without influence on government was clearly demonstrated in the 1976 riots. Time and again, informal leaders were able to mobilise young blacks to riot or strike, but these same leaders were then unable to gain any attention from the government for black demands. Formal leaders, the government insisted, spoke for urban blacks. This pattern of non-communication becomes increasingly difficult to break constructively.

Black-black ethnic-based conflict or black-black conflict between the employed and the unemployed cropped up occasionally in the urban unrest of 1976 and 1977. Bloody clashes took place between migrant workers (Zulus in Soweto and Xhosa in Langa) and students over student demands for work boycotts and the closing of *shebeens* — the illegal drinking places. Such clashes will occur again, given the social encapsulation of migrant workers from the surrounding community of the township and the strong pressure to hold on to any job during the long-term South African depression. But it would be a serious miscalculation to take comfort in these cleavages. In the longer-run, the entire black industrial population — including migrant workers and their families left in homelands — is participating in an incipient, but massive regional economic, social, and political revolution. Independent homelands will contribute to the political socialisation of migrant workers and their families, so the urban-rural cleavage will shrink, rather than expand. This likelihood makes even more important the development of an informed, articulate, and respected formal leadership among blacks.

Should South African society continue to nurture siege cultures with their dogmatic and exclusive nationalisms, a major racial confrontation would be certain in the not-too-distant future. Such an outcome to centuries-long black-white coexistence in Southern Africa would be disheartening to all but the most politically-naive and reckless.

THE FUTURE OF THE RACE SUPREMACIST ETHOS

Any serious consideration of possible future changes in Southern Africa must take into account the impact of the race supremacist ethos. Can this ethos ever be eliminated? A cynical view suggests that the task involved is tantamount to 'washing an ethiope white' — that is, doing the impossible. More rigorous examination of the fate of racist beliefs, behaviour, and attitudes elsewhere suggests that, at most, a shift takes place from either dominative racism or aversive racism to meta-racism.[27] As in the U.S., when constitutional and legal supports for dominative and aversive racism are ended, such racists find it increasingly difficult to maintain their behaviour patterns. Their continued need to maintain racial superiority is converted into terms of class superiority, which partly disguise continued racist attitudes and behaviour — or meta-racism.

Jacques suggests convincingly that a 'fantasy social structure' underlies racist behaviour. The interplay between fantasy social structure (or unconscious) and manifest social organisation (believed to be rational) must be grasped if the endurability of racism is to be comprehended.[28]

Thus, in any society, the rational justification for social values, norms, and institutions is buttressed by an irrational, unconscious set of values and norms. The dialectical relationship between social reality and social fantasy aids understanding of both a racist social structure and racist individuals.

Changing racist attitudes and behaviour can be extremely difficult, even when radical changes are made in the institutions sustaining racism. Why is this so? While it is generally true that any social structure is the embodiment of the deepest human concerns, needs, attitudes, symbolisation, and unconscious conflicts — the sum of the subjective universe about each individual — in racist cultures, and with racist attitudes and behaviour, the primacy of these subjective factors is the strongest.

Social and political activists usually ignore the primacy of the subjective in their preoccupation with practical means and ends, but, nonetheless, their radical positivism can be constructive in creating the social and material dis-equilibria necessary for the dismantling of racist institutions. Once these institutions are gone, meta-racism begins to show itself.

The greatest danger posed by the transition to meta-racism is the substitution in the racist individual of a consciousness of class superiority for the earlier consciousness of racial superiority. But the racist, like the conversion hysteric or the hypochondriac, masters of symptom substitution, remains enslaved to the primacy of the subjective and his own unconscious. He is like a spider trapped in his own web.

The anxiety of racist individuals confronting potential structural change in racist cultures provides a fascinating opportunity to see the primacy of the subjective at work. Anxiety and even primitive fears emanating from the collective racial and cultural unconscious are understandable. They are even a reasonable response, when drastic revolutionary change threatens the survival of privilege, power, and hegemony by a previously-superordinate group. But where the demand is limited to 'peaceful' change, however radical its rhetoric, the anxieties are often much greater than the situation deserves.

Why is this so? The unconscious not only prefers metaphor to objective reality and a dialectically ambivalent attitude toward reality, it also holds an obdurate preference for hyperbole. How else account for the superordinate threat of the gun when the subordinate offers the olive branch? In listening to and being guided by his unconscious, the racist — in the grip of an intoxicating delusional system — begins to believe that real death is preferable to the horror of metaphysical death — the elimination of his racial fantasies. Although the material and psychological consequences of this subjective fixation are often dehumanising to both his victims and himself, the racist holds to his subjective values. He has a kind of childhood disease. Like all humans a product of his socialisation experiences, the racist has not outgrown his childhood fantasies about magic, narcissistic self-idealisation, and personal omnipotence — all of which centered about race, because of parental values and experiences.

The supposedly-adult racist nonetheless can surprise or even shock the observer with claims, actions, and pronouncements during crises which equal those of a developing child. Racial arrogance? A projection of personal omnipotence? Belief in the innate superiority of whites and white culture and civilisation? Narcissistic self-idealisation? Even magical thinking — the suspension of larger events to meet personal preferences — seems central to the frequent racist comment that Rhodesian or South African blacks either have no interest in political power or no capacity for it. Will they wait a thousand years, or even a hundred, or even a generation? Only in child-like, racist magical thinking.

The assault on the race supremacist ethos is now international in scope, and because of that, optimism is in order about the global elimination of racist institutions. Dealing effectively with meta-racism will remain a more difficult problem. It will be necessary to develop social institutions capable of linking up with the fantasy social structure of the society so that racist fantasies will diminish in fervour and persistence. This will not be easy anywhere, especially in South Africa.

THE "ECLIPSE OF REASON"

The questions raised in this analysis are central to the social-psychological circumstances and prospects of South Africa. Yet for them to be thought about, debated, and resolved, South Africans of all colours and all shades of political opinion must unmask the 'eclipse of reason' — the irrationality — which dominates South African public life.

One of the cardinal difficulties in unmasking the eclipse of reason in this volatile group conflict situation lies in the diabolic ability of the superordinate-subordinate social structure — in its preoccupation with the maintenance of social-political equilibrium and its concern that marginal change might turn uncontrollable — to stifle systematically individuals and groups who, in the longer-term at least, could prove beneficial to the society. Whatever short-term gains in stability, the long-term cost in political rationality is much greater.

Merleau-Ponty says that a society's public life should be evaluated on the basis of whether or not it is guided by a public, formal morality of principles.[29] What is a formal morality of principles? Here I repeat emphatically what I have written elsewhere:

> Quite simply, it is the kind of morality in which principles such as those of justice and liberty are publicly defended in the absence of a just social order and free men and women.[30]

Paradoxically coexisting with the eclipse of reason in Southern Africa is the embryonic triumph of a formal morality of principles. A new order demands that the gap between these formal principles and objective social conditions be rapidly narrowed.

REFERENCES

1. Morris Merleau-Ponty, *Humanism and Terror, trans.* J. O'Neill (Boston: Beacon Press, 1969).
2. G. Wiendieck, 'The Behavioural Relevance of Ethnic Attitude Studies,' *Social Dynamics* (Cape Town) 1, no. 2 (1975), pp. 125-142.
3. Marshall W. Murphree, 'Sociology and the Study of Race: Contemporary Perspectives for Southern Africa,' *Social Dynamics* 1, no. 2 (1975), pp. 111-124.
4. David Welsh, 'Social Research in a Divided Society: The Case of South Africa,' *Social Dynamics* 1 no. 1 (1975), pp. 19-30; and Henry Lever,

'Some Problems in Race Relations Research in South Africa,' *Social Dynamics* 1, no. 1 (1975), pp. 31-44.

5. Murphree, 'Sociology and the Study of Race'
   Also see. Manganyi, *Being-Black-in-the-World* (Johannesburg: Sprocas-Ravan Press, 1973), p. 8; and Philip Mayer, 'Class, Status, and Ethnicity as Perceived by Johannesburg Africans,' in Leonard Thompson and Jeffrey Butler, eds., *Change in Contemporary South Africa* (Berkeley and Los Angeles: University of California Press, 1975).

6. Mayer, 'Class, Status, and Ethnicity;' Lawrence Schlemmer, 'Black Attitudes: Adaptation and Reaction,' paper to the Association for Sociology in Southern Africa, Kwaluseni, Swaziland, 1975; S. Biesheuvel, 'The Influence of Social Circumstances on the Attitudes of Educated Africans,' *South African Journal of Science,* July 1957; and Melville Leonard Edelstein, *What Do Young Africans Think?* (Johannesburg: South African Institute of Race Relation, 1972).

7. Donald G. Baker, 'Race and Power: Southern African Race Relations in Comparative Perspective,' paper to the Association for Sociology in Southern Africa, Kwaluseni, Swaziland, 1976.

8. D. Kruger, *Psychology in the Second Person* (Grahamstown, South Africa: Rhodes University, 1975), pp. 11, 12.

9. Murphree, 'Sociology and the Study of Race.'

10. Characterisations of South African blacks by whites often attribute to them docility, apathy, compliance, and hedonism. Although the adaptive utility of these and similar attitudes in the face of overwhelming alienation and dehumanisation is sometimes noted, the falseness of the consciousness expressed in these attitudes is often overlooked. I argue elsewhere that this false consciousness is in reality intermediate between a subjective ambivalence — the violent reverie (fantasy) — and violence as a social act under propitious revolutionary conditions. See *'The Violent Reverie': in this collection.*

11. Manganyi, cited in *Rapport* (Johannesburg), 25 April 1976, pp. 3, 4.

12. D. Kruger, 'Die Ondergang van die Afrikanerdom?' (The Downfall of Afrikanerdom?), *Deurbraak* (Cape Town) August 1976, pp. 9-11.

13. Manus Buthelezi, 'The Christian Challenge of Black Theology': paper to the Black Renaissance Convention, 1975.

14. Donald G. Baker, 'Race, Power, and White Siege Cultures,' *Social Dynamics* 1, no. 1 (1975), pp. 144-45.

15. Buthelezi, ibid.

16. J. Degenaar, 'The Concept of a Volksuniversiteit,' paper to the Conference on the Role of Universities in Southern Africa (Cape Town, 1976), pp. 2, 3.

17. H. J. Brinkman, 'Comments on the papers of Professor J. Degenaar and Professor T. van der Walt,' Conference on the Role of Universities in Southern Africa, p. 2.

18. Erik H. Erikson, *Dimensions of a New Identity* (New York: W. W. Norton and Company, Inc., 1974).

19. Philip Mayer, 'Class, Status, and Ethnicity,' p. 153.

20. Ibid.

21. Marshall W. Murphree, 'Sociology and the Study of Race,' p. 113.

22. Henry Lever, 'Some Problems in Race Relations Research in South Africa,' pp. 36, 37.

23. Lawrence Schlemmer, 'Black Attitudes: Adaptation and Reaction.'
24. cf. Black statements to this effect appear invariably to be banned in South Africa. Thoahlane Thoahlane, ed., *Black Renaissance;* (Ravan Press, 1975) and Thoko Mbanjwa, ed., *Apartheid: Hope or Despair for Blacks?,* Black Viewpoint no. 3 (Durban: Black Community Programmes, 1976).
25. Donald G. Baker, 'Race and Power,' pp. 19, 20.
26. Ibid., p. 6.
27. J. Kovel, *White Racism: A Psychohistory* (New York: Vintage Books, 1970).
28. Elliot Jacques, 'Social Systems as Defense Aginst Persecutory and Depressive Anxiety,' in M. Klein, et. al., eds., *New Directions in Psychoanalysis* (New York: Basic Books, 1955), pp. 478-498.
29. Morris Merleau-Ponty, *Humanism and Terror.*
30. Manganyi, 'Reassessment Towards a New Consensus on Migratory Mine Labour' (Johannesburg: Proceedings of the International Consultation on the Role of the Church among Migrant Mine Workers, 1976).

Universalism, Particularism and Africanisation

The theme of this essay is a problem of increasing importance for the future and well-being of higher education in Southern Africa. There are extant in South Africa today competing traditions and conceptions of what a university should be in a plural society. I hope to show that South African universities have failed to respond creatively to the challenge of being *African* universities. This they have done by opting for either a sterile universalism or an ethnoparticularism. An alternative to these conceptions is suggested and discussed.

Current concepts of the Academic Ethos

In the Southern African context (I use Southern Africa advisedly), what, we may ask, is a university? In other words: is there an overriding consensus about the character, aims and functions of universities as institutions of higher learning? Let me suggest with due emphasis that the answer to the second question is a decisive negative. Such an unfavourable outcome to the question carries with it a number of significant implications for what I choose to describe as the *confidence crisis* in Southern Africa's universities.

Sociologists and politicians use different language to express the view that in Southern Africa we live in the midst of a plurality of languages, cultures, ethnic and racial groupings. Perhaps even more important in real terms are differences of a political and ideological character which in their contest for ascendancy will help determine the destiny of the subcontinent.

The legacy of this cultural, racial-ethnic and political plurality in as far as universities and the academic ethos are concerned is the existence of three main conceptions of what universities are and should be (ideally) in the context of a plural society. Before I proceed to a brief discussion of these trends, I want to direct attention to a uniquely South African phenomenon in relation to the definition of a university. No university in South Africa is a university without further qualification. It is, as matters stand today, an English, Afrikaans or Xhosa university. The university in South Africa is ethnically particularistic in a sense which is crudely contradictory to the universalistic ethos which is one of the defining features of the traditional, that is, classical notion of what universities should be.

A study of the ongoing but sporadic debate involving the nature and functions of universities in South Africa reveals, *inter alia,* that:

(a) The English language universities in South Africa believe themselves to be more in line with the ethos of universities in the western world, that is, they claim to emphasise *universalism,* autonomy and 'academic freedom' as opposed to an insular *particularism.*

(b) The Afrikaans language universities on the other hand are said to be defined volksnationalistically as *volksuniversiteite* and are by the same token more *particularistic* in orientation although Viljoen (1976) has disputed the legitimacy of this characterisation. The Black universities in as much as they are a product of current thinking and government policy have been conceived volksnationalistically with a view to making them into ethnic universities. (Degenaar, 1976).

(c) The third conception of universities is not specific to South Africa in that it has been much more clearly articulated in Middle rather than Southern Africa. (Murphree 1976, Wandira 1976). In this instance the emphasis is on 'pragmatisation' and 'Africanisation,' two notions which are discussed later.

Regarding the universities for blacks, one should add immediately that there has been over the first half of the present decade a black perspective on what universities should be even though this particular point of view has tended to suffocate under the intellectual debris of the customary South African debate on universities and academic freedom. So although in South Africa a particularistic African point of view about universities has not yet been avidly and clearly articulated for various reasons, it is the potential force of this conception, among other equally important factors, which has created the crisis in black universities during the present decade and earlier.[1]

The existence of competing conceptions of the university ethos has a decided bearing on black universities particularly in respect of student-staff (administrations included) relations on the one hand and the academic ethos prevailing at these universities on the other. Before the implications of this situation are stated explicitly, it is necessary to present in outline some of the main assumptions underlying the three competing conceptions and traditions considered above.

The Universalistic Perspective

Since all universities are social institutions they are in all instances relatively particularistic in that they have to satisfy to varying degrees the requirement for societal relevance. In broad terms though and in practice, it seems that a particular university ethos may favour the predominance of either a particularistic or universalistic orientation. Clearly the universalistic ethos is the older of the two and has its origins in the medieval concept of university. Writing about these orientations in the context of the University of Rhodesia, Murphree (1976:6) has this to say:

> This reference to conceptions considered to be of universal applicability points to the core of the dimension of conflict we are now considering. The twin objectives of Africanisation and Pragmatisation are both 'particularistic' in that they address themselves to specific sectional or regional requirements and realities. A given society will expect its university to set about fulfilling these objectives from the same particularistic perspective, often restricted to the problem-solving mode, or, if latitude is given to permit a contribution to the definition of goals, solely on the basis of some particular ideological dogma. Such a particularism is, I believe, antithetical to the genius of the university tradition and inimical to its viability and ultimate

93

utility. At the core of this tradition is a universalistic ethos in so far as it adduces a normative pattern of action of universal applicability. This normative pattern attaches to the elevation to axiomatic status, in the university tradition, of the constructive and enriching potential of rationality. This is the general principle of universal validity: whatever is rational — regardless of its source or implication — is admissable as a basis for the academic enterprise; whatever is irrational — regardless of its attraction or apparent necessity — is not. It is in this sense that I refer to the university tradition as being 'universalistic.'

However, it is important, as James Moulder (1976) has pointed out, not to confuse a statement of ideals for a description of real conditions and events. Yet it is true to say that the English-medium universities in South Africa believe themselves to be more universalistic than their Afrikaans-medium counterparts.[2] I think that academics in South Africa need to ask: is universalism in the South African context a realistic ideal? I think not and I will try in a latter section to show why this concern with universalism is empty and unpromising in the short run and what types of ideals need to be set for all South African universities to meet the challenge of the times in which we live.

A Local Version of the Particularistic Perspective

Two recent papers by two leading Afrikaner academics (Degenaar: 1976; Viljoen: 1976) suggest that Afrikaans-medium universities are particularistic, Degenaar being more convinced of this fact than Geritt Viljoen. This particularism, so Degenaar believes, arises from the notion of a *volksuniversiteit,* itself a part of the wider context of Afrikaner *volksnasionalisme.* Degenaar (1976: 17-18) summarises his conclusions regarding the concept of a *volkuniversiteit* and related concepts as follows:

> In my analysis of the concept of *volksuniversiteit* I introduced the model of volksnasionalisme as a starting point and explored this concept of a university by means of a family of words used by the protagonists of this notion. This family of words consisted of the following members: *volksuniversiteit, volksgebondenheid, volksdiens, Christelik-Nasionaal* and 'interested community'. An analysis of these concepts revealed

that within this model the university is described mainly on an ethnocentric basis. This has important implications for the interpretations attached to words such as individual, volk, community, society, university and state ... The university is an institution of higher education in the heart of the volk and cannot be described except in terms of its being necessarily bound to the ethnic group which it is called to serve.

The existence of this family of words is one indication of the significance for Afrikaner nationalism of the concept of a *volksuniversiteit*. An examination of this family of words reveals another heuristic feature, namely that the concepts themselves are highly emotive or, more explicitly, evocative. Take the case of *volksgebondenheid,* translated by Degenaar to mean 'ethnocaptivation'. That this concept is evocative may not be disputed on reasonable grounds. In any case a dynamic and growing nationalism could hardly be expected to be devoid of a working terminology of this kind.[3]

According to this ethno-particularism the university, like the Church, must have a sense of dedication, mission and *above all a calling*. It, the university, is an instrument of the *volksiel:* the interested community.

When this model of a university is examined on an abstract level it indeed may appear to have merit. This is not surprising since as an ideal it shares in the glory of the idealism of a growing nationalism. Were South Africa an ethnically and racially homogenous society, the chances are that this model of a university would thrive without serious threat to its cultural hegemony. South Africa is heterogeneous in several respects and it is this fact which needs to be reckoned with in considering the ultimate value of an ethnocentric particularism in the definition and running of universities. In the South African context, therefore, an ethnocentric particularism is as unpromising as the universalistic model of the English-medium universities.

African Universities: 'Pragmatisation' and 'Africanisation'

Africanisation and pragmatisation are two concerns which constitute the distinctly African perspective in relation to the particularism of universities on the African continent. In spirit if not on detail, Wandira (1976) would agree with Murphree (1976:3) who describes Africanisation in the following terms:

> By 'Africanisation' is meant not simply the indigenisation of the staff of African universities — although this is of course an important aspect of the process — or even the adaptation of curricula to African cultural and social contexts. The search for Africanisation is a more embracing quest which lays upon the African university the task of assembling the entire gamut of African heritage and ensuring its continuity by an analysis and pedagogy which gives it a contemporary relevance to the needs and aspirations of the modern African nation-state.

On the other hand, the requirement for 'pragmatisation' is best exemplified by an extended statement produced after the 1972 Accra Workshop (Yesufu, 1973; cited by Thompson, 1976):

> In the decade of the 1960's, African countries saw in universities the intellectual foundation, and the source of the high-level manpower to sustain the newly-won Independence. Modelled upon foreign institutions, however, the universities have not manifested the degree of flexibility essential to meet the needs of the common man. The emerging university of the 1970's in Africa, must, therefore, shed its foreign forms and cloak; it must not just pursue knowledge for its own sake, but for the sake of, and the amelioration of the conditions of life and the work of the ordinary man and woman. It must be fully committed to active participation in social transformation, economic modernisation and the training and upgrading of the total human resources of the nation. Even in the pursuit of its traditional functions of promotion and dissemination of knowledge, as well as research, the university must place emphasis on that which is immediately relevant and useful.

It has since become clear that the university not only in Africa but in Western Europe and North America has recently come under scrutiny. This scrutiny has arisen as a result of the chronic conflict of ideals between those that have become traditional to universities and populist values and demands for egalitarianism. The so-called 'Ivy-League' Universities such as Yale and Harvard in the United States have been under pressure to abandon eliticism and meritocracy in their selection and admission policies.[4] If the question of relevance, that is, a form of particularism, is being advocated for established universities in fairly well established liberal and developed democracies, it should come as no surprise if particularism in the sense of social and historical relevance becomes a major consideration in the models of universities to be developed for Africa.

Discussion thus far has provided a mere outline of the major perspectives which have a significant bearing on the general academic ethos particularly in African universities. It need hardly be emphasised that such a confluence of perspectives turns out to be of less effective significance in the case of English and Afrikaans-medium universities in South Africa. This is clearly understandable since in both instances tradition either in a particularistic or universalistic direction has been developed over time. In addition, there is no significant discrepancy between the manner in which Afrikaans-medium universities define themselves and the aims and prospects of Afrikaner nationalism as a volknationalism.

The University and the Four Estates

Black universities (including those for Indians and Coloureds) like their Afrikaans-medium counterparts were conceived and created Volksnationalistically except for the fact that *political ethnicity* (on which they are based) as part of an overall national policy is much narrower and limited when compared say to Afrikaner nationalism. In a sense these institutions are diminutives of the powerful *volksuniversiteite* supported as the latter are by a powerful nationalism. The difference between the *volksuniversiteite* and the black ethnic universities arises mainly from the historical contexts within which they came into being. A study of the national debates which accompanied the establishment of Stellenbosch University, the University of Pretoria or more recently the Rand Afrikaans University reveals that the impact of Afrikaans *volksnasionalisme* was not only strong but also clearly articulated.[5] On the other hand, the black universities came into being accompanied by nothing more than an anguished whimper on the part of the black population of South Africa. To state this historical observation differently, we need to say that since there is evidence to show that in places such as Soweto *political ethnicity* is being edged out by a decidedly *black ethnicity* (Mayer: 1975) there can be no congruence between African aspirations and the character and aims of African universities as they exist today in South Africa.

Discussions of universities often suggest an implicit assumption to the effect that universities are corporate institutions which may be characterised as particularistic or universalistic. In reality, the situation is often far from ideal in that the four estates of a university (students, academics, governing council and 'the powers') may be at variance to such an extent as to be in concealed or open conflict.

I single out for special consideration the confidence crisis in student-staff relations within the context of the ethno-particularism of African universities. The sources of this crisis must be related to two crucial factors amongst others. The one contribution to the crisis arises from the fact that since these universities are in conception at least diminutives of the Afrikaans *volksuniversiteite,* a major inspiration that has determined their character is the particularistic perspective of the Afrikaans-medium universities. It seems reasonable to assume also that since until recently most of the academics and administrators in the African universities came predominantly from the *volksuniversiteite,* they would be informed in their discharge of their academic responsibilities by the particularistic ethos and aims described earlier.

Most African students in the 1970s may be expected to know and acknowledge more than the Van Wyk de Vries Commission of Inquiry into universities was prepared to admit, namely that for a plural society such as South Africa there could never be one and only one legitimate concept of university. (cf. Degenaar: 1976). I think that the confidence crisis and the crucial element in the consequent conflict involving the four university estates arises from a latent and sometimes overt conflict of aspirations. The most deep-seated aspirations of a people often achieve creative expressions as a nationalism. At the level of aspirations, the conflict involved is one between a nominal ethnic nationalism (political ethnicity) as against a potentially broader South African nationalism.

Within the context of Africanisation of all segments of South African society such as is to be suggested in this discussion, a broadly based nationalism may be transformed from the status of a receding mirage into a potentially enriching reality. I return to the issue of Africanisation at a later stage.

To the existing competing images of universities and the conflict of aspirations as these latter express themselves as nationalisms must be added another factor of importance. I am referring to the demand of the academic ethos for universities, university teachers and students to dedicate themselves to the search for truth — a search which is founded on a belief in the value of and human capacity for rationality. A university community which is not saddled with latent conflicts and mistrust can survive any crisis which arises from a rational and intellectual difference of opinion. Where students are thwarted in their desire to develop an inspiring identification with their teachers and university, we often find that academics themselves are not only insecure but lacking in dedication to the search for and advancement of knowledge. Intellectual life — academic life — does not begin and end in the safe security of lecture halls. If academics have serious problems in the rendering of their academic responsibilities such difficulties should not be of their own making. In Southern Africa in particular, academics need to develop a kind of frontier out-look which transforms difficulties into fertile opportunities.

We can realise this last objective by creating for the university tradition and ethos some built-in safe-guards which should be monitored and reviewed from time to time. Universities are required by the very character of their place in national life to maintain a lively and continuing commitment to reflection on what it is that the university and university education are about. There must come to the fore within universities a deep-rooted concern about the quality of human relationships for it must be remembered that even societies may be evaluated on the basis of the prevailing quality of human relationships. The 'genius' of the university tradition (to use Murphree's term) consists mainly of a dedication to rational and open inquiry. Needless to say, this value even in the particularisms of Southern Africa needs to be elevated to the status of a valuable dogma.

Universalism, Particularism and Africanisation

I want to begin here with the identification of a *need* and proceed to a formulation of a challenge. The need is for universities in Africa to develop a character and role that is more in line with African conditions, that is, conditions in Africa in the past, the present and the future. With regard to the past we need only add here that Africanisation as a peculiarly African particularism must make the reinterpretation of the African past possible. The critical issue for Africanisation is relevance — the need for universities in Africa to be rooted in the Africa of the twentieth century and the future. For the university, Africanisation means innovation and adaptation, within the framework of a tradition which means that wise and realistic limit-setting with regard to change must prevail over indifference.

Prof. Murphree has this to say about Africanisation (Murphree: 1976:3):

> By 'Africanisation' is meant not simply the indigenisation of the staff of African Universities — although this is of course an important aspect of the process — or even the adaptation of curricula to African cultural and social contexts. The search for Africanisation is a more embracing quest which lays upon the African university the task of assembling the entire gamut of African heritage and ensuring its continuity by an *analysis and pedagogy which gives it a contemporary relevance to the needs and aspirations of the modern African nation state.* (Emphasis added.)

In the context of African universities (including white African universities) Africanisation must come to mean pragmatisation on a more inclusive level. Several implications are suggested here for a relevant 'analysis and pedagogy' for universities in Southern Africa. But first, we need to raise and deal with the following question.

Is it meaningful to think in terms of Africanisation for the white universities of Southern Africa?[6] I think that there is a real need to think along these lines even within the context of political uncertainty about the future of the subcontinent as a whole. As white South Africa emerges from its delicate and fragile identification with Western Europe into new yet unclear identification with Africa, new demands will emerge on the intellectual horizon. An opportunity is presenting itself in this regard for a creative scholarship in the interests of Africanisation involving all the universities of Southern Africa. The quest, it seems to me, should be for a more inclusive humanism, Africanism and the creation of a new identity predicated on an informed and dispassionate assessment of our heritage. The black universities, on the other hand, may promote their Africanisation efforts by deciding whether they become more African by exclusion of other South Africans rather than by their inclusion. Africanisation must mean more than indigenisation since the former refers more specifically to a frame of mind quite apart from the enthralling objectivity of skin colour. In the analysis and pedagogy required by Africanisation, the African academic must come to depend more on an inner freedom — a freedom unleashed from unconscious inhibitions and fears of one kind or another. In a variety of ways, Africanisation and pragmatisation are relevant to South African universities and the future of the larger heterogeneous society of which they are a part.

Striving for a beneficial and positive particularism, universities in Southern Africa must fulfil at a most distressing time in the history of the region the value of universalism primarily in the limited sense of an 'insistence on rationality'. This means that the 'cognitive superiority' (cf. Shils: 1976) of the academic profession must come to mean more than an intellectual eliticism of a socially unproductive kind. Universalism and particularism are values which constitute part of what Shils describes as the 'academic ethos'.

By insisting on Africanisation and pragmatisation for all universities in Southern Africa, I have in effect placed into question the two main competing conceptions of universities which support the white universities in South Africa. Is universalism as professed by the English-medium universities a realistic option for current and future South African conditions? Secondly, is the ethnocentric particularism of the Afrikaans-medium universities and those for blacks for that matter a viable option? If sentimentality is excluded from the examination of these questions, the answer to both questions is no! To begin with the first of these questions one should admit that what the advocates of universalism in South Africa are entitled to under present circumstances is idealism — certainly nothing more substantive than that.

It must be admitted that universalism (the practice of values attached to universalism) is incongruent with the values of a *limited politics* as well as sectional and competing nationalisms. For a nation state to support the universalistic perspective of its universities it needs to have gone a long way towards being a participatory democracy with a firm constitutional and historical foundation. What seems to have happened in the history of higher education in South Africa is that the English-medium universities have steadfastly dedicated themselves to the ideals of autonomy and academic freedom. In doing so, they have in their dedication to these values mistaken the descriptions of these values as ideals for real possibilities and in this way have not reacted creatively to the conceptual challenge which faces South African universities today. This challenge does not consist only in indigenisation of students and staff but in a fuller recognition of the socio-historical context within which English-medium universities exist today. Like the universities for blacks and Afrikaans-speaking South Africans, the 'open universities' must become African universities by adopting a philosophy of Africanisation. The need for Africanisation exists. The challenge has to do with the conceptual work which needs to be undertaken to make Africanisation a reality. The quest for Africanisation requires of English-speaking South Africans that they cultivate a healthy identification with Africa, that is, begin to experience and believe themselves and future generations of white South Africans to be Africans. Needless to say that the worship of false gods is not a monopoly of the English-medium universities in their idealism. The Afrikaans-medium universities in their ethno-particularism (advocated though it is as a South Africanism) must also come to terms with the limitations of the concepts of *volksuniversiteit* and *volksnasionalisme*.

The demand for Africanisation means that universities in

South Africa and the subcontinent as a whole have to make a dramatic move away from a preoccupation with the ideals per se of universalism or an ethno-particularism, captivating though these may be. Africanisation in the evolution of the academic ethos of the region must precede commitment to universalism. I said that universalism is an unrealistic ideal in the context of a limited politics such as we have in some parts of Southern Africa at the moment. By the same token it can also be said of the particularism of the *volksuniversiteit* that such a sectional and limited approach proves unequal to the challenge of ethnic and socio-cultural plurality which is currently the hallmark of communities in Southern Africa today.

A strategy for Africanisation derives its major momentum from existing conditions while its inspiration arises from a more realistic anticipation of the future. Among others, the important aspects to be recognised meaningfully for Africanisation to become a force in higher education and in the context of prevailing conditions, the following are worthy of note. First, there must emerge on the cultural, political and spiritual levels an invigorating confidence in the future of the African continent. In the new African identity that should emerge from an imaginative resolution of the problems of Southern Africa there should exist no need for the special protection of particular cultural identities. Cultural systems provided they are viable and healthy enough are capable of protecting themselves against less established and more volatile systems. This should mean that any cultural system or identity which requires special measures for its continued vitality, that is, is dependent on factors other than its own vitality and internal directing mechanisms to survive, is hardly worth having. This should apply to all identities and cultural systems including, for example, those of Africans and Indians in South Africa.

It is more profitable in the long run to accept the consequences of this truth than it is to be forced into an uncomfortable 'a ha' experience in the face of unpredictable political, economic and social disruptions of one variety or another.

On the one hand, Africanisation must become for the

countries of Southern Africa a popular social movement of such magnitude as to transform the white people's ambivalence about their identification with this continent into a new willingness to be 'naturalised' as it were. The condition for such a naturalisation of white Africans is, amongst others, acceptance of the truth that no identity or culture worth its salt requires special protection. Such an outlook creates a climate for new patterns of human relationships and must surely affect in fundamental ways the political and economic structures supporting the current superordinate-subordinate symbiosis characteristic of race relations on the subcontinent.

The challenge for the universities is that for their 'cognitive superiority' to be historically and socially meaningful, they must anticipate the historical outcome suggested above. This means that in their admission policies, selection policies and scholarship the universities must begin to take their location both in place and time into significant consideration.

New Directions for an old Controversy

When extant conceptions of a university are examined in the context of cultural, ethnic and racial plurality in Southern Africa they turn out to be unequal to the complexity of the social, economic, political and future demands of the African continent of which they are a part. In the context of Southern Africa today with its limited politics and competing nationalisms, the universalistic perspective suffers from being too aristocratic a notion of a university apart from being too idealistic in the light of local conditions. Also idealistic in an almost opposite direction is ethno-particularism which suffers mainly from being too sectional a perspective for the kind of future which looks likely in the long run.

While it may be the responsibility of career politicians to do the impossible, the job of universities seems to be that of making certain that only through rational inquiry is the impossible brought into the ambit of reality. Although it may be said that universities in South Africa, for example, are 'under siege' as one observer alleged, it remains true to say that such a status should not preclude the development of imaginative approaches to the problems of universities within the region. As I see it, Africanisation is the response and approach with the greatest promise for the future not only of higher education but for the region as a whole. Only one who believes himself to be a Messiah can prescribe the actual mechanics of how Africanisation should be brought about. My main objective in this discussion has been to identify the need for new directions of thought in the debate about the nature and functions of universities in South Africa. Needless to say a belief system has to be developed in advance of serious concern with problems of application.

NOTES

1. See G. M. Nkondo: *Turfloop Testimony* (Johannesburg: 1976).
2. See G. van N. Viljoen: 'The Afrikaans Universities and Particularism' (Cape Town: 1976) for a discussion of this theme.
3. It is my view that all nationalisms in their evolution develop a working vocabulary often of an evocative kind. Recently, the black consciousness movement in South Africa, for example, brought in its train a family of words such as 'black', 'non-blacks' and so on.
4. In the United States pressure on the universities has been legitimised and legalised in the Federal policy of *Affirmative Action* which prescribes the desirable distribution of minorities such as Afro-Americans and women in university faculties.
5. See J. Degenaar: 'The Concept of a Volksuniversiteit' (Cape Town: 1976) and G. van N. Viljoen: *Ibid.*
6. It is significant that some students in the Nusas camp of South African student activity are beginning to talk and think Africanisation.

REFERENCES

DEGENAAR, J. 1976. 'The Concept of a Volksuniversiteit.' Cape Town: Conference on the role of Universities in Southern Africa. Mimeographed.

MOULDER, J. 1976. 'University Neutrality: Some puzzling reflections in a South African Mirror.' Cape Town: Conference on the role of Universities in Southern Africa. Mimeographed.

MURPHREE, M. W. 1976. 'Universalism, Particularism and Academic Freedom: The Rhodesian Case.' Cape Town: Conference on the role of Universities in Southern Africa. Mimeographed.

NKONDO, G. M. (Ed.) 1976. *Turfloop Testimony:* Johannesburg: Ravan Press.

SHILS, E. 1976. 'The Academic Ethos.' Cape Town: Conference on the role of Universities in Southern Africa. Mimeographed.

THOMPSON, L. 1976. 'Some Problems of Southern African Universities.' Cape Town: Conference on the role of Universities in Southern Africa. Mimeographed.

VILJOEN, G. van N. 1976. 'The Afrikaans Universities and Particularism.' Cape Town: Conference on the role of Universities in Southern Africa. Mimeographed.

WANDIRA, A. 1976. 'The special tasks and problems of the "One-County-One-University" institution in Middle Africa.' Cape Town: Conference on the role of universities in Southern Africa. Mimeographed.